# BLUEBERRY PEACHES, RED ROBIN PIE

*An Annotated Cookbook of Mississippi Gulf Coast Recipes*

## STELLA LA VIOLETTE
### and
### Paul Estronza La Violette

Illustrated by Stig Marcussen

Waveland, Mississippi

# BLUEBERRY PEACHES, RED ROBIN PIE

Published by Annabelle Publishing
Post Office Box 87
Waveland, MS 39576

Library of Congress Catalog Card Number:
2001091929

ISBN 0-9673936-5-5

987654321

First Edition

Printed in the USA by
**WIMMER**
The Wimmer Companies
Memphis
1-800-548-2537

*Blueberry Peaches, Red Robin Pie*

# TABLE OF CONTENTS

# *OPENERS*

*A FEW WORDS TO START ... PAUL*

*SOME REMARKS ABOUT MY RECIPES AND
COOKING IN GENERAL ... STELLA*

# A FEW WORDS TO START

 $\mathrm{T}$ oday is Saturday, and I'm writing in the back office while Stella is wade fishing over by Carrere's pier. It's a division of chores. I write; she gets the food for the table. Jennie our Weimaraner is sleeping by my feet, and some hummingbirds are darting about a feeder near the window.

In its way, this book is about our division of chores; Stella gets and prepares the food, I spend a great deal of time enjoying eating what she prepares, Jennie stays patiently nearby, hoping something will drop, and the birds circle about, eating the things that bird eat and keeping us company.

It's a nice way for us to split the work of living and, as you have probably noticed, a lot of it with us has to do with food. I'm not sure about the birds, but to Stella, to Jennie and to me, food is more than a necessity, it is part of the amusement, the art, the joy of the good life we lead.

This is essentially a cookbook in which Stella has assembled recipes of different dishes that she likes to prepare and I like to eat. To add to the flavor of the recipes, I have included stories about the foods she talks about, ourselves, Jennie, the regional birds and the Mississippi Gulf Coast in general.

Many of the stories are old stories that I have told before, but they are nice stories, worth repeating, and they are pertinent to what we are writing about in this book. I have arranged these additions so that they relate to the particular group of recipes that Stella presents; sort of a Greek chorus accompaniment.

There is more to my involvement than that, however. What has been exceptionally nice is that while Stella has had the task of checking each recipe, I have had the fun of taste testing them in what has been for me a parade of superb meals.

I hear the pickup pulling in. Stella's back and if I'm lucky she'll have caught a small black drum, a fish I particularly like. If she has, we'll have it as a late breakfast with some yard eggs, fried tomatoes and onions from the garden. If there is roe, I'll have that fried with the fish. I hurry to the garage to help her unload. She'll think I'm being nice, but like Jennie, I know when to wag my tail.

She's full of chatter, showing me two nice speckled trout that she says will be perfect for our brunch. She slaps the fish on her fillet board and in minutes has them filleted and is heading to the outside shower. As she goes, she tasks me to run over to Pass Christian to get some large shrimp and a fresh loaf of French bread.

I leave with Jennie in the pickup. I guess I'm spoiled. Years past, when I was a bachelor, shopping for my week's food consisted of buying seven TV dinners, some bread, butter, tea and yogurt. What was bad was that I didn't know there was a difference.

Stella, who was a fair cook when we were first married, started to expand her skills when we moved south and built a house on the beach of a small town on the Mississippi Sound. Stella found she was able to wade fish in front of the house, grow vegetables in the back and buy many of the other things she needed from the farmers' market or from the workboats in one of the local marinas.

She began doing things in our kitchen with these fresh foods in an intuitive way that constantly surprised me. The meals she prepared became at first, very good, then great, then excellent. And my palate improved.

Jennie and I cross the Bay St. Louis Bridge and we're in Pass Christian. We buy the bread, still warm, at the bakery, then go to get the shrimp on the Pass's pier. Some shrimp boats have come in and there is a noisy bustle as they unload. I find that the shrimp a little high, four dollars a pound, but they are about a twenty count (twenty shrimp to the pound), which is very good, and I get a pound.

When I return, I find Stella has cooked some wild rice and made a salad with tomatoes from her garden and some excellent balsamic vinegar. I set the table in the dining room, while she finishes fixing the meal.

First she butterflies and seasons the shrimp and then pan-fries them with the fish in virgin olive oil, placing the results on a large platter with the rice and fried eggs. One of the fish did have some roe and she includes that as a little lagniappe on the side.

We sit down to eat, looking out the large windows at the place where much of the food on the table was caught. The show of the food on the platter in the center of the table is delightful to see and mouth-watering. I uncap a dark heady beer, put my bare feet on Jennie's back (she's under the table; maybe something will fall), and enjoy a good meal. The birds are at the humming bird feeder, all appears right in our particular part of the world.

So, as you try the recipes that Stella has written in our book, I will try to entertain you with stories about Stella and Jennie and myself and, on occasion, a few of the birds and our other friends.

(A word about my chapter stories / remarks; I often mention some food or dish in them. In most instances when I do this, there is a recipe for that particular food or dish in that chapter or, if not in that chapter, in other parts of the book.)

### *...PAUL*

# SOME REMARKS ABOUT MY RECIPES AND COOKING IN GENERAL

*The* recipes I have included in this book are, for the most part, easy to prepare. Few take more than an hour, most only about three quarters of an hour. Don't be put off by this, you will find as you try them that they result in excellent dishes.

Their ease in preparation stems from my having to spend much of the week in a government office. Thus, our evening meals have to be easy to prepare and over the years I have adapted my cooking to suit this weekday limitation. My secret is to keep them easy to prepare, but good to eat. According to the rather critical judge I have living with me, Paul, I have succeeded.

Meals on weekends are a little different. I can, on those days, spend more time doing what I really enjoy, puttering around the kitchen, trying different things and preparing more elaborate meals. As a result, the recipes I give in the book for these days take a little more preparation, but not much more.

From experience, I have found that good meals don't have to be overly elaborate and I have modified my cooking accordingly. For example, sauces. I believe that all too often recipes act as if the sauce is the recipe's main ingredient and that the entrée is secondary. My philosophy is that a sauce is a garnish whose purpose is to enhance an entree's flavor, rather than smother any original taste it might have. The sauces I present in my recipes follow that philosophy.

(When Paul and I are in a restaurant that completely drowns the entrée with their "special" house sauce, we wish that they followed this philosophy as well.)

In all my recipes, I have tried to stick to the basic idea that if you start off with good food and be careful how you fix it, then the results will be a good meal.

*I'm no stranger to trying different things and different ways to make those things, but I always follow the cardinal rule that good fresh food should give you great dishes.*

*By this I mean using fresh vegetables in season and fresh meat rather than frozen meat whenever possible. I advocate that, when the recipe calls for certain ingredients, don't use artificial substitutes; use real whipping cream not a canned imitation; use real vanilla, not artificial vanilla; use butter, not oleo, etcetera. Of course, there are times and circumstances that may require a compromise, but in essence, stick with this simple rule of using fresh, real ingredients in your recipes.*

*In this book, you will find that a set of three oysters,*  *, means it is a recipe we particularly like. If there are two of these sets together it is a recipe we are in love with. When you see a frog, it will be the start of a remark or a hint about that particular recipe. Two frogs mean that what follows is a particularly significant hint.*

*Finally, and this is most important, I hope that you, like myself, enjoy cooking. Cooking is as entertaining to me as going to a good movie is to others. The recipes I have included in this book are recipes for meals that I enjoy making and that Paul and I enjoy eating. I hope you will as well.*

*Bon appetit!*

**...STELLA**

# *APPETIZERS AND SALADS*

| APPETIZERS | SALADS |
|---|---|
| *OYSTERS BIENVILLE ala Stella* | *"NEW" POTATO SALAD* |
| *SPICED PECANS* | *SPINACH SALAD* |
| *BRUSCHETTA ala Espana* | *GARDEN FRESH TOMATO SALAD* |
| *PÂTÉ* | *CORN SALAD* |
| *CRANBERRY MEATBALLS* | *CHILLED BABY PEA SALAD* |
| *GORGONZOLA CHEESE SPREAD* | *CUCUMBERS IN SOUR CREAM* |
| *BOURSIN CHEESE SPREAD* | *CUCUMBERS WITH OLIVE OIL AND VINEGAR* |
| *DRIED BEEF CHEESE BALL* | *GREEK SALAD* |
| | *FRENCH HONEY MUSTARD DRESSING* |

# A FEW POTTED CRABS

W hen my neighbor's pier was in fair shape, we would put two or three crab pots down among the pier's pilings. We'd put them in late Friday and by Sunday noon we'd have about eight good size crabs that would make a good lunch. During the week, we would get a few each evening. Stella would steam these and we would have them as appetizers to our meal.

Coast people like to boil their crabs, seasoning them with a New Orleans spice called "Zatarain's." They often have propane gas burners for cooking them outside; placing large pots on these low set gas units and, bringing the seasoned water to a boil, dump the crabs in as needed for a crab boil in the back yard. Potatoes or corn are often thrown in to make the results a nice backyard feast.

Stella prefers to steam our crabs the way they do around the Chesapeake Bay: with lots of salt, a little water or beer in the bottom of the pot, and use a Baltimore seasoning, "Old Bay," as the seasoning. One advantage of this is that little water is needed and the pot can be cooked inside on a kitchen range.

This is handy during the week when we want crabs as part of our evening meal. Stella cracks and cleans the crabs in our deep kitchen sink, and serves them at the table as a sort of antipasto.

There is very little mess. Stella thinks our way is the better of the two. "Not as soggy." But I'll eat crabs cooked either way.

My neighbor's pier is gone except for a group of small pilings and we on occasion put our pots among these. But things have changed.

What with the casinos, there are more people living here than before and more come on weekends. There are more people on the beach and wading in the water. When they come across our pots, they poke or lift them and later, when we come, we find them upended or the crabs released.

When our grandchildren started coming down to visit us in the summer, we'd put a crab pot out for them. The two girls thought it was great fun. But it soon became apparent that people were messing with the pot. We weren't catching any crabs.

We were a little frustrated. We didn't want to ruin the girls' time with us by standing and monitoring crab pots, yet the girls were obviously looking forward to catching some crabs.

Finally, I had an idea! I would "salt" the pot! Without their knowing it, I would sneak off and buy a dozen or so crabs. Then when Stella got the girls in the back of the house with some excuse, I would go out and fill the pot full of crabs.

The pot would be so full it would seem absurd, but then what would they know (and we needed at least a dozen for lunch)? Later, toward noon, we would send the girls out to check the pot and the screaming when they returned was delightful.

What was amazing was the time I put in twelve and they brought back fourteen.

### *... PAUL*

# MY APPETIZER
# AND SALAD RECIPES

*P*aul is right, I do use Old Bay as seasoning for my seafood instead of the favorite of most of the locals, Zatarain's. But my use of it is really a matter of habit, from my cooking when I lived in the greater metropolitan DC area. I believe that both are very good and you should make your own choice on what to seasoning to use.

The appetizers and salads I have included in this chapter point up the difference between the preparations I make for a holiday meal or dinner party and a weekday meal I'm prepare for just Paul and myself. In my recipes, I try to show that difference. Simple changes or additions can often make a plain, but otherwise excellent meal, appear to be something extra special, even elegant. Many of the appetizers I have included in this chapter are great for doing just that.

As with most of this book, the ingredients of my appetizers' generally reflect the cuisine of the Mississippi Gulf Coast: oysters, shrimp, pecans and whatever our local markets or the Sound has in season at the moment. These ingredients, like my using Old Bay instead of Zatarain's are a balance of what you like and what is available when you are preparing the recipe. You are quite welcome to and actually should pick and choose among the ingredients unless the recipe is very specific in its list of ingredients.

Note that in this chapter, I don't present a recipe for a green salad. I think that anyone can come up with such a salad quite easily without my giving a recipe. However, I would like to make a few general remarks on such salads. I prefer romaine rather than iceberg lettuce. The romaine seems to me to retain its crispiness better than iceberg.

Also, I like to use balsamic vinegar in my green salads (and, in fact, in most of my salads). Balsamic vinegars are nice in that there are many different kinds (and prices) that offer a variety of flavor and intensities.

*Blueberry Peaches, Red Robin Pie*

   *Just a few drops of balsamic vinegar adds a great deal of flavor to your dish. It is particularly good on fruit salads and enhances meat and cooked vegetables. So, it is extremely versatile; experiment with it to find out how you like to use it best. You will be surprised at the things you end up using it on.*

   *One important note as to salads: please don't treat your salad as an added chore like peeling a potato, that is, the quicker it is done the better. Take time and care with it as you do any other element of the meal. If you can't do this for some reason, then omit the salad entirely from your menu.*

   *Let me expand on that thought a little further as it is important to the thoughts that go with the recipes in this book: never think of the entrée as the only important ingredient of the meal you are preparing.*

   *All of the meal's components, whether soup, side dish or salad are critical parts of the  balance in flavors that you are trying to bring to the meal. None should be thought of as being so minor that the care in their preparation can be short changed. As with the salad, if for some reason you can't take the required care of a particular component of the meal, then omit that component from your menu*

   *The salads I have included in this chapter are examples of the importance I feel salads hold as part of a complete meal. I have made them simple and easy to prepare. Some of the simplest, for example the cucumber salads are amazingly wonderful taste treats. Their secret is using fresh ingredients, good dressings, such as a good oil and a choice balsamic vinegar and keeping the salad cool (usually chilled) until ready to serve.*

**... STELLA**

**17**

# APPETIZERS ...............
## OYSTERS BIENVILLE ala Stella

### Sauce

½ lb. shrimp,
Old Bay or Zatarain's shrimp boil
½ cup salted butter (1 stick)
1 cup scallions, finely chopped
¼ cup parsley, minced
1 ½ tsp. garlic, minced
½ cup flour
½ cup heavy cream
1 ½ cups milk

4 large egg yolks, beaten
¼ cup sherry
1 tsp. salt
1 tsp. white pepper
½ tsp. cayenne
1 cup fresh mushrooms
1 box rock salt

### Topping

3 tbsp. Romano cheese
3 tbsp. Parmesan cheese

3 tbsp. bread crumbs
½ tbsp. salt

Boil shrimp in a highly seasoned shrimp boil, cool, finely dice and set aside. Melt butter in a heavy saucepot over low heat. Add scallions, parsley, and garlic and cook until soft. Stir in flour and mix thoroughly. Add cream and milk. Continue stirring until smooth. Add egg yolks, sherry, salt, pepper, and cayenne. Cook until mixture thickens. Add finely chopped mushrooms. Cook for 2 minutes more. Add shrimp. Cook for 3 minutes more or until sauce becomes thick.

Place in glass container and refrigerate for 2 hours.

When ready to serve, place about 2 dozen scrubbed oyster shells on bed of rock salt. Place an oyster on each shell and cover with a tbsp. of sauce. Grate cheeses and combine with breadcrumbs and ½ tsps salt. Sprinkle a tsp. of mixture on each oyster.

Bake in 500-degree oven for 15 minutes or until oysters are well browned on top.

Serves 4.

*Since this is a dish I prepare fairly often, I reuse the oyster shell. To clean them, I soak them in warm water after each use, and then scrub with a stiff vegetable brush, rinse and put out in the sun to dry. Afterwards, I store them in zip lock bags for the next time.*

*This is an excellent recipe and its success is due to the highly seasoned shrimp whose rich flavor is carried over to the sauce. You can also expand this recipe into an entrée by using it as a casserole dish (omitting of course the oyster shells). In this case the oysters are laid in a casserole dish and placed in the oven as before. The result is served with a little rice or pasta on the side and some French bread for dipping. And don't forget a nice green salad. Appetizer or entrée; in either case this is a great party or guest dish and is a definite crowd pleaser.*

\*\*\*\*\*

## SPICED PECANS

1 egg white
¾ cup sugar
2 ½ tbsp. water
1 tsp. cinnamon
½ tsp. salt

¼ tsp. allspice
¼ tsp. clove
¼ tsp.  nutmeg
8 cups pecans

Whisk eggs whites until they are thoroughly broken up. Add remaining ingredients and continue whisking until all are incorporated. Spread on a cookie sheet sprayed with vegetable oil.  Bake for 55 minutes in 175-degree oven.  Cool and store in sealed container.

This makes a nice munchy appetizer.

\*\*\*\*\*

**19**

## BRUSCHETTA ala Espana

| 1 large fresh tomato | Salt and pepper |
|---|---|
| Basil, fresh | 1 loaf of crusty bread |
| 3 or 4  cloves of garlic | Romano cheese, shredded |
| Olive oil | |

Scald, peel, seed and chop the tomato.  Finely chop basil and garlic.
Heat a tablespoon of oil in a skillet and add the tomato, garlic and basil.
Cook slowly until ingredients become soft and dry out somewhat.
Season with salt and pepper.

Slice bread in about 1 inch  slices.  Toast on both sides under broiler.
Drizzle small amount of oil on each slice.  Spread tomato mixture on
top and add some shredded cheese.  Pop bread back in broiler and let
cheese melt slightly.

Serve immediately while still hot. Serves 6 to 8.


*This is a well-liked Mediterranean snack that is nice to serve
when you are not having a meal. It's a variation of a popular
antipasto most people call Bruschetta.  Bruschetta, also known as
Roman garlic bread, is normally made with olive oil and garlic only.*

*You will probably find a hundred different variations of the recipe, all
are excellent. My combination is a mixture of an Italian and Spanish
variation.  The Spanish version has the bread first toasted and then
rubbed with fresh garlic followed by a fresh, seeded tomato and olive
oil.*

*****

# PÂTÉ

| | |
|---|---|
| ¼ lb. butter | 1/8 tsp. cinnamon |
| 1 large onion, diced | Salt and pepper |
| 1 lb. chicken livers | 1 oz brandy |
| ¼ tsp. nutmeg | Romaine lettuce leaves, fresh |

Melt butter slowly in a large skillet. Add onions to skillet and cook slowly - *do not brown*. Wash, drain chicken livers and add to butter / onion mixture. Continue cooking slowly until livers begin to brown slightly. Add nutmeg, cinnamon, salt and pepper to taste. Add brandy and cook another minute.

Cool mixture slightly and process in blender until smooth. Strain through fine strainer and pour into one or two well-buttered molds or terrines. Chill for at least 8 hours. Set the molds in warm water to loosen and turn out on a bed of Romaine lettuce. Serve with crackers or toasted French bread.

Makes a little over one quart.

*For variation, you can add cooked bacon or onion bits to the Pâté. Mix in just before placing in mold. If placed in a tight container, pâté keeps under refrigeration for three to four days very nicely. Much longer than that and it starts to discolor. So, watch how much you make. The amount presented here is for a party.*

*In addition to being an appetizer, pâté makes an excellent breakfast dish - the pâté spread on toasted crusty French bread, some fresh fruit and tea or coffee will satisfy your morning appetite.*

**\*\*\*\*\***

## CRANBERRY MEATBALLS
### (Party Recipe)

| | |
|---|---|
| 1½ lbs. lean ground beef | Salt and pepper to taste |
| ½ lb. ground pork | Tabasco |
| ½ cup finely diced onion | 1 can whole cranberry sauce |
| 1 small clove garlic crushed | 1 can tomato sauce |
| 1 egg | 1 cup beef broth |
| ½ cup Italian bread crumbs | |

Mix ground beef, pork, onion, garlic, egg and bread crumbs thoroughly. Add salt and pepper to taste as well as a dash or two of Tabasco. Form meatballs with a small ice cream scoop and place on a baking sheet. Bake in 350 degree for about 15 to 20 minutes. Turn meatballs periodically in order to get a good crusty coating on all sides.

Combine the cranberries, tomato sauce and beef broth and cook for about 15 minutes. Add the meatballs and cook very slowly for approximately another 30 minutes. Chill and refrigerate. Reheat just before serving.

 *These can be made in advance and kept very nicely for three to four days under refrigeration. They can also be frozen very effectively and made a week or so in advance of a party or gathering.*

\*\*\*\*\*

## GORGONZOLA CHEESE SPREAD

**2  8 oz. packages of cream cheese    6 oz. Gorgonzola cheese**
**½ cup unsalted butter**

Bring all ingredients to room temperature. Blend cream cheese and butter together until mixture has a smooth consistency.  Add Gorgonzola and mix by hand. Allow to stand at room temperature for one hour to allow a full blend of flavors.

Chill for 1 hour and serve.

 *This makes a very nice spread for crackers or slightly toasted French bread.  But, it's at its best when accompanied by fresh grapes, apples or pears.  Green grapes dipped one by one into the spread are delicious.*

*\*\*\*\*\**

## BOURSIN CHEESE SPREAD

**8 oz. of whipped butter**          **1 tsp. fresh dill weed**
**1 lb. of cream cheese**            **½ tsp. dried marjoram**
**2 small cloves garlic, minced**    **½ tsp. dried basil**
**¼ tsp. ground clover**             **½ tsp. chives**

Let butter and cream cheese soften to room temperature and then add and mix herbs. Allow to stand at room temperature for one hour to allow a full blend of flavors.  Pack in a small crock and chill overnight. Serve with French bread or crackers.

*Both of the above recipes make excellent spreads to use either as appetizers or as a light breakfast served with fresh fruit and coffee or tea. Use an attractive plate to add to their presentation.*

*\*\*\*\*\**

## DRIED BEEF CHEESE BALL

**2  8 oz packages cream cheese**
**6 oz dried beef**
**3 scallions**
**1 cup chopped pecans**

Bring cream cheese to room temperature.  Chop dried beef and scallions.  Cream the cheese until smooth and add beef and scallions. Mix thoroughly and chill for at least one hour or until cheese can be rolled into a ball.  Roll in chopped pecans and serve with various crackers or breads.

*This makes a good appetizer for a party when you want your dinner guests to keep busy while you are finishing putting the late touches on the meal.*

*****

# *SALADS* ...................

### *"NEW" POTATO SALAD*

| | |
|---|---|
| **3 lb. new potatoes (red or white skin)** | **¼ tsp. celery seed** |
| **½ cup chopped celery(strings removed)** | **Salt and pepper to taste** |
| **1/3 cup chopped sweet onions** | **¾ cup Kraft Miracle** |
| **3 sweet gherkins, quartered, sliced thin** | **Whip (no substitute)** |
| **2 eggs boiled, chopped** | |

Boil potatoes until you can just pierce them with a fork. Drain and let cool (they will continue to cook while cooling). Peel or leave the skins on and cut into inch cubes. Add celery, onions, gherkins, and eggs to the potatoes. Season with celery seed, salt, and pepper to taste. Fold Miracle Whip into mixture making certain not to mash ingredients together. Serve just after preparation while still slightly warm or chill in refrigerator for one hour.

Serves 8 to 10.

*When I say "new" potatoes, I'm talking about the potatoes that are available in early spring and have a thin skin that can be easily slipped off after they are cooked*

*I can't help it, I love this salad and make it at the slightest excuse. The thing I enjoy most about it is the chunks of flavor you get when the ingredients are not over mixed. I find the gherkins and the Miracle Whip give the salad a little more flavor than traditional mayonnaise.*

\*\*\*\*\*

25

# SPINACH SALAD

## Salad

| | |
|---|---|
| 5 oz. fresh spinach | 2 hard boiled eggs |
| 1 med. sweet onion (red skin if possible) | 4 slices of bacon |
| | Salt and pepper to taste |
| 4 med. sized fresh button mushroom | |

Stem, wash and dry spinach and tear into bite-sized pieces. Slice half of the onions into 1/8" slices and separate into rounds. Slice mushrooms and set aside. Boil eggs, then cool and slice. Fry bacon until crisp, cool and finely chop. Place spinach in large bowl. Add onions, mushrooms and toss. Just before serving, toss with dressing (see below) and season with salt and pepper to taste. Garnish with eggs and bacon and serve.

## Dressing

| | |
|---|---|
| 1 tbsp. sugar | ½ cup light olive oil |
| 3 tbsp. hot water | 2 tbsp. apple cider vinegar |

Melt sugar in hot water and cool. Add oil and vinegar and whisk until combined. This will make a very good sweet-sour dressing and will enhance the various flavors of the salad.

Serves 4.

 *Red skinned onions add a pretty color to the salad, but they must be sweet, otherwise the onion flavor will overpower the salad. If you can't get the red, Vidalia or Texas sweets will do.*

 *To avoid that dark ring on the yolk of a hard-boiled egg, place the eggs in a pan of cold water with enough water to cover the eggs. Bring the water to a boil and immediately remove from heat, cover and let stand for 17 minutes. Immediately immerse the eggs in cold water and peel. There should not be a yolk line and the white should be tender instead of tough. Best of all, you don't have to waste time worrying about the pot boiling over.*

*****

## GARDEN FRESH TOMATO SALAD

| | |
|---|---|
| **1 clove of garlic** | **Olive oil** |
| **2 large fresh "just-out-of-the-** | **Salt and pepper to taste** |
|    garden" tomatoes | **Dash of balsamic vinegar** |
| **1 med. sweet onion** | |

Slice garlic in half and rub the sides of a glass or wooden salad bowl. Discard garlic. Slice tomatoes and onion into ¼" slices and place in bowl. Dress tomatoes and onion with 2 to 3 tbsps. of olive oil. Season with salt and pepper and let marinate at room temperature for one hour. Chill an additional hour and serve.

Serves 4.

 *You are in for a real treat — marinating the tomatoes forms a lovely natural juice that markedly adds to the dish. This salad is wonderful served with nothing but French bread for dipping in the sauce and a tall glass of iced tea.*

*The acid in the tomatoes should negate the need for any vinegar. However, you will find that a dash or two will add to the general taste.*

*****

## CORN SALAD

1½ cups freshly cooked corn or
   1 can white shoepeg corn
1 small cucumber, peeled,
   seeded and diced
1 small tomato, peeled, seeded
   and diced

¼ green pepper, diced
3 scallions, chopped
Mayonnaise
Vinegar
Salt and pepper
Romaine lettuce leaves, fresh

Mix all ingredients together and dress with the mayonnaise. Season with salt and pepper and a dash of vinegar to taste. Chill for at least two hours. Serve on a bed of Romaine lettuce leaves.

Serves 4.

\*\*\*\*\*

## CHILLED BABY PEA SALAD

2 cups fresh baby peas or
   10oz box frozen baby peas
1 tbsp. sweet onion, finely
   chopped

3 tbsps. mayonnaise
Dash of vinegar
Romaine lettuce leaves, fresh
Strips of red pepper

If fresh peas are used, cook and chill. Defrost frozen baby peas and keep them chilled. Add the onions, mayonnaise and a dash of vinegar and fold together thoroughly. Salt and pepper to taste. Serve on a fresh lettuce leaf along with a strip of red pepper for color.

Serves 4.

 *It is important to keep the peas chilled for the best flavor. Paul loves both of the above salads but this one especially. I think he would be happy to eat it as a meal by itself.*

\*\*\*\*\*

## CUCUMBERS IN SOUR CREAM

3  cups peeled, sliced cucumbers
¼  cup chopped fresh dill or 2
    tbsps. dry dill weed
½  med. onion thinly sliced

¼  cup sour cream thinned with
    milk
Pinch of sugar
Salt

Mix all ingredients and thoroughly chill before serving.  Season lightly with salt when serving.

Serves 4 to 6.

\*\*\*\*\*

## CUCUMBERS WITH OLIVE OIL AND VINEGAR

5 or 6 small pickler cucumbers
Olive oil
Balsamic vinegar

Salt and pepper to taste
Fresh dill

Wash cucumbers and score with a fork.  Then slice and dress with olive oil and balsamic vinegar.  Chill until ready to serve.  Season with salt and pepper and some fresh dill.

Serves 4.

*Both of these salads are excellent when these fresh small cucumbers are in season (especially if they are from your own garden). Try to only use these small cucumbers; this does make a difference.*

*What is especially nice about these salads is that they are so simple to fix! Scoring the cucumbers gives them a nice presentation for the table.  It is important to keep them cool in order to retain their crunchy crispiness. The fresh dill adds a unique freshness to the mixture.*

\*\*\*\*\*

## GREEK SALAD

1 clove garlic, sliced in two
3 cup lettuce in bite-sized pieces
1 small cucumber, sliced
1 med. tomato, cut in small
   wedges
1 med. green pepper, sliced
   in rounds

6 to 8 ripe olives
½ cup crumbled feta cheese
½ tsp. freshly chopped oregano
Olive oil
Apple cider vinegar
Salt
Freshly ground black pepper

Rub a salad bowl with the garlic halves. Discard garlic. Add lettuce to bowl and toss lightly to blend garlic oils and lettuce. Add cucumber, tomato, green pepper, and olives to bowl. Again, toss lightly. Chill until ready to serve. Just before serving, add feta cheese, oregano, oil and vinegar to salad and toss. Season with salt and pepper and serve.

Serves four .

*****

## FRENCH HONEY MUSTARD DRESSING

¼ cup cider vinegar
1/8 cup water
½ cup olive oil

3 tbsps. honey
2 tsps. prepared Dijon
mustard

Whisk all ingredients together until light and fluffy. Taste and make adjustments to suit your taste. Chill and serve. Shake dressing vigorously each time you use it so that the ingredients are thoroughly mixed.

 *This is very good served with a green salad or a combination salad. It is also particularly good with a fruit salad, but you may want to increase the amount of honey used according to your personal preference as well as to accommodate the fruit used in the salad.*

*****

# SOUPS

**STELLA'S OYSTER CHOWDER**
**POTATO LEEK SOUP**
**BLACK BEAN SOUP**
**GAZPACHO**
**JAMBALAYA SOUP**
**CREAM OF SPINACH SOUP**

# SOUP OF THE EVENING, BEAUTIFUL SOUP!

*Beautiful Soup, so rich and green,*
*Waiting in a hot tureen!*
*Who for such dainties would not stoop?*
*Soup of the evening, beautiful Soup!*
*Soup of the evening, beautiful Soup!*
(*The Mock Turtle's song*)

The Mock Turtle's song to Alice was sung with tears in his eyes, but, of course, we all know those were mock tears. Because soup, good soup, does not produce tears; soup is a joy to the eye, to the meal, and, above all, to the stomach.

Let's be clear on one thing before we go any further. The soup I am talking about here is soup made from scratch, not canned or packaged just-add-water soup. And, luckily for me, Stella makes great soup! Excellent soup! Wonderful soup!

Over the years I've traveled more than a bit, and have had the pleasure of having enjoyed some very good food in a number of very different places. I've found that the most enjoyable of these dishes are those made from a mixture of local things, added when they are fresh and at their very height of flavor.

Paella is a good case in point. In Spain, the contents of a good Paella varies with the season and even with what part of the country you are in. The recipe changes, but the basic components that make it so very good: fresh, local ingredients, are always the same.

We on the Mississippi Sound are blessed with an abundance of what can honestly be described as great seafood; no make that fantastic seafood; seafood that half the country would give their eyeteeth to have and, in fact, go through a lot of trouble to get. That's a fact! Next time you are in Pass Christian, drive down North Street and see you what you find.

Parked beside the seafood shipping facilities will be large refrigerator trucks with Maryland, Delaware and Virginia license plates. Listen! Hear that! These trucks will have their engines running.

They're waiting for oysters! When loaded, each of these large trucks will shift into high gear, hit I-10 and make a non-stop speed run to deliver fresh oysters to restaurants in some oyster-starved northern city.

Think about it. These people will be eating our oysters! Oysters from oyster shoals out in the Mississippi Sound with wonderful names such as Merrill Coquille, Square Handkerchief and Tail of the Square Handkerchief.

When in season, fresh crabs and shrimp caught in the Sound move north from the Coast in much the same way, in the back of these large trucks. But we fool those northern rascals; we eat all we can of those oysters, those shrimp, and those crabs before we let what's left get away.

I can picture some confused soul sitting at a long butcher paper-covered table at Captain Drinks Crab House near the end of Highway 3 in southern Maryland, cracking open crabs thinking he's eating Chesapeake Bay crabs.

Not so, baby duck! Those crabs came direct to you from Pass Christian, Mississippi in the back of one of those refrigerator trucks.

We are equally proud of our fish. Yes Sir!! Oh the thoughts of redfish, white sea trout, flounder, black drum, mullet, speckled trout... What is particularly nice is that all of these oysters, these crabs, these shrimp, these fish, all of these, make great soups, wonderful soups.

Which is good. Because great soups say a lot about the people of an area and their cuisine. One of the principles of judging a good restaurant that Stella adheres to is the quality of their soup. Her theory is that if the chef will take time and care to make a good soup, he/ she will take time and care with the rest of the meal.

I've found that this is an excellent rule of thumb; one that has steered me to some fantastic meals. Good soup, good meal. Here on the Coast, great soups abound and the best are soups made from seafood still dripping wet from being pulled out of the Mississippi Sound.

As I write this, it's the end of December. A degree or so near freezing is the highest temperature we are going to have today. Now is the time for hot soup and what is better than a fish- or shrimp-based soup? You don't know? Well I'll tell you. An oyster chowder.

Oyster chowder is good! Oh heavens, yes! Give me good oyster chowder and I'll let you have our cat, Holly, to keep you company for a week. Give me some of Stella's oyster chowder, and I'll let you keep the cat.

Not only is it the end of December, it is New Year's Eve and you are probably wondering how best to start this new year. Well I know you are going to be busy tonight, but tomorrow, get yourselves some oysters and the fixings and follow the chowder recipe Stella has included here.

I promise you that as sure as this is going to be a great year, you will enjoy yourself.

*... PAUL*

# REMARKS ON MY SOUP RECIPES

*I love making soups. They're a little bit like an adventure in that they are so easy to modify to fit an occasion or a whim or whatever you might have on hand.*

*But there is more to it than that. Despite each recipe's precise list of ingredients, I am constantly surprised by the variation in taste a soup I prepare one time has with the soup I prepare from the same recipe, another time. I suppose this has to do with the fact that we use natural ingredients that vary in quality and ripeness. All this does is instill in a cook such as myself the realization that we must constantly taste the food as we prepare it whether it be soup or salad.*

*There is one secret to remember in making good soups. That is that many improve with age! Letting these soups sit overnight allows them to blend the flavors of their ingredients. The longer they sit, it seems, the tastier they get. This doesn't apply to all soups, but for the many that it does apply to, it is a secret to keep in mind.*

*Another secret to remember, is that the basic recipes for some soups are very versatile. The Oyster Chowder that Paul has made such a fuss over can be easily made into Clam Chowder or Fish Chowder. Or you can leave these out altogether and make an excellent Potato Soup!*

*The other soups I've included are the same way; they can be easily changed. Have fun! Experiment. Think of making soup as if they all originated from the same basic recipe as Rock Soup. Remember that recipe? "First take one rock, Place in boiling water. Add other ingredients as available. Allow to simmer till ready. Remove rock and serve."*

### ...STELLA

## STELLA'S OYSTER CHOWDER

| | |
|---|---|
| ¼ lb. butter | 1 can chicken broth |
| 1 cup chopped onions | 1 can whole kernel corn |
| 1 large bay leaf | 2 – 3 cups milk |
| 2 – 3 tbs. flour | 1 qt fresh oysters and their |
| 2 large potatoes | liquor |
| 2 large carrots | 1 cup heavy cream |
| 2 large stalks celery | Salt, white pepper and cayenne |

Melt butter over low heat in a heavy soup pot. Add onions and bay leaf and sauté until onions are translucent. Remove bay leaf. Add flour to mixture and make a light roux. Set aside.

Peel and dice potatoes in one inch pieces. Slice carrots and celery in quarter-inch slices. Cook all in broth until tender. Add corn. Use additional broth or water if more liquid is needed to properly cook vegetables.

Add roux to vegetables and stir until completely combined. Return to burner over very low heat. Add milk, oysters and their liquor. Continue to cook over low heat until oysters are heated and their edges become slightly curled. Add cream, salt, white pepper and cayenne to taste. Continue to heat until cream is heated. Be careful not overheat and curdle soup.

Makes four to six servings.

*This is truly a suburb chowder! It goes best when served with French bread and unsalted butter. And remember with only a slight variation in the main ingredient, it can be made into a clam or potato chowder.*

\*\*\*\*\*

## *POTATO LEEK SOUP*

4 tbsps. butter
1 ½ cups thinly sliced leeks
   (white and some green)
¼ cup minced onion
1 large clove garlic, minced
3 tbsp. minced carrot

4 cups chicken broth
1 ½ cups diced potatoes
½ cup heavy cream
Salt and pepper to taste
Chives or dill, fresh

Melt butter in a heavy pot over a low heat. Sauté leeks, onion, garlic and carrots in the melted butter until leeks are soft. Do not allow to brown. Add broth and potatoes, cover, bring to a boil and lower heat. Simmer until potatoes are tender.

At this point, you can puree the mixture or leave it as is. Add the cream and reheat, but do not boil. Season with salt and pepper. When serving add a dab of sour cream and a sprinkle of fresh chives or dill. If soup is too thick, thin with more broth or half-and-half cream.

Makes four to six servings.

 *This soup can be served either hot or cold. Both ways are good and each has its own distinct characteristic.*

 *The dab of sour cream and a sprinkle of fresh chives or dill when serving not only make a good presentation, it adds markedly to the taste*

\*\*\*\*\*

## BLACK BEAN SOUP

1 lb. dried black beans (soaked overnight)
10 cup water
2 tsp. salt
6 tbsp. olive oil
1 cup minced onion
1 cup minced bell pepper
¾ cup minced celery and leaves
¾ cup minced carrots
2 cloves of garlic, minced
1 tsp. ground cumin
1 tbsp. white vinegar
1 tsp. Maggi's seasoning
Salt and black pepper to taste
Minced onions
Sieved hard boiled egg yolk

Cook beans in water and salt until soft. While beans are cooking, sauté onions, bell pepper, celery and carrots in oil until onions are brown. Add garlic, cumin, vinegar and Maggi's seasoning. Cook, stirring for about 3 minutes.

Drain a little water from the beans and add to vegetables. Cover and cook vegetables slowly for 30 minutes. Combine with beans, adding more water if needed. Reheat and adjust seasoning with salt and pepper.

Makes six to eight servings.

 *After serving the soup, pass bowls of minced onion (soaked in olive oil and vinegar) and sieved egg yolk for garnish. Not only do these add to the presentation, they come at just the right moment to give the soup the best flavor from each of these very different garnishes.*

*****

# *GAZPACHO*

| | |
|---|---|
| 1 clove garlic, cut in half | 2 tbsps. olive oil |
| 3 cups peeled, seeded, finely chopped tomatoes | 2 tsps. lemon juice |
| 1 cucumber, peeled, seeded and chopped | 1 tsp. salt |
| 4 tbsps. minced green pepper | ¼ tsps. white pepper |
| ½ cup chopped sweet onion | 1 dash Tabasco sauce |
| | 1 cup chilled tomato juice |
| | ¼ cup chopped parsley |
| | 1/2 cup sour cream |

Rub a mixing bowl with the halved garlic. Leave the garlic in the bowl. Add tomatoes, cucumbers, green pepper and onion and mix well. Add the olive oil, lemon juice and seasonings. Stir well and chill for at least 4 hours. Before serving, add the chilled tomato juice and mix thoroughly. Top with chopped parsley and a tbsp. of sour cream.

Makes about six servings.

 *Gazpacho is a summer soup with many variations. The one I've given here is the one Paul and I like. The main secret to making all of the varied recipes for this excellent soup is the use of garden fresh vegetables at their peak of ripeness. It is a very refreshing, light meal in the hot summer and it helps you make use of all those vegetables in your garden. Feel free to vary the ingredients to suit whatever is at the peak of ripeness in your garden or available at the farmers' market.*

 *Remember that the longer this particular soup sits, the tastier it gets. I usually make a large container and keep it for a week at a time.*

\*\*\*\*\*

# JAMBALAYA SOUP

1 lb. Polish sausage
1 qt. water
1 large chicken breast (full breast)
1 can chicken broth (28 ounce size)
1 can whole tomatoes
1 large green pepper
1 large onion
2 stalks celery
1 cup okra, sliced
1 fresh or dried cayenne pepper
½ cup rice
2 small zucchini squash
salt and pepper

Slice Polish sausage in bite-size pieces. Place water in a large soup pot, add sausage and cook on medium heat until it becomes a light broth. Chop chicken in bite-sized pieces and add to pot along with chicken broth and tomatoes and cook additional 5 minutes. Chop pepper, onion and celery and add to pot. Add corn, okra, cayenne pepper and rice. Cook for 20 more minutes. Add zucchini and cook until zucchini is cooked every so slightly. Season with salt and pepper to taste.

Serve immediately with crusty corn bread and a lettuce salad. Serves 4.

 *This, as opposed to gazpacho, is excellent on a cold winter day. This is a very hearty soup, yet it is light, in that it has very little fat. It keeps very well, and is also better the next day. Crusty bread with salt free butter and a green salad round out the meal.*

\*\*\*\*\*

# CREAM OF SPINACH SOUP

½ cup butter
1 med. onion, finely chopped
1 to 2 tbsp. flour
4 cups chicken broth
1 lb. spinach, washed and chopped

1 cup heavy cream
salt and white pepper
Freshly ground nutmeg

Melt butter in a heavy stockpot.  Add onions and cook until translucent, but not browned.  Add flour and make a roux.  Gradually add chicken broth. Stir until smooth.  Add spinach and cook for two to three minutes until wilted .  Gradually add heavy cream and stir until smooth.

Season with salt and white pepper and serve. Serves 4.

*This is an excellent selection for the first course of any meal. It is especially nice both for looks and taste for a dinner party. For a nice presentation on such occasions, serve in shallow soup bowls with a bit of freshly ground nutmeg.  The nutmeg greatly enhances the delicate taste and presentation of the soup.*

*****

*Stella and Paul La Violette*

# *SEAFOOD*

*BAKED REDFISH COURTBOUILLON*
*TROUT AMANDINE ala Stella*
*CRABMEAT QUICHE*
*FRESH TUNA STEAK SALAD in a garden*
*BLACKENED "ANY FISH"*
*STUFFED FLOUNDER*
*FRIED SOFT-SHELL CRABS*
*STEAMED CRABS (Eastern Shore Style)*
*CRAB CAKES*
*TARTAR SAUCE*

# BIG SHRIMP, FAT OYSTERS and BLACKENED FISH

We usually get our shrimp directly from the boats at the docks in the Pass or from the boats in our own Bayou Caddy. They are nice to have fresh like that, right off the bought that caught them. It's one of the little extras that make living on the Mississippi Coast so nice.

If large enough, 20 or so count, Stella likes to season, butterfly and cook them on the grill with onions, green peppers and zucchini squash. Smaller shrimp, 30 to 50 count, are good for dishes like gumbo. Stella, however, finds that while it may be pretty to have all those little shrimp, it is too much work to behead and peel them and she prefers to use the larger 20 to 25 count shrimp.

As to oysters, although we usually buy ours already shucked, the neighbors occasionally have a shucking party of a sack of oysters. This is a fun way to spend a weekend evening during the fall or winter. Whatever is left is used the next day to make oyster po'boys — New Orleans French bread sandwiches.

Po'boys can be stuffed with just about anything, including shrimp and fish. I like my oyster po'boy with the bread just slightly toasted to make it crisp, then buttered and the oysters piled on; and don't forget the Crystal or Tabasco hot sauce. Stella lists Tabasco as the hot sauce ingredient in her recipes, but either sauce is nice to use.

Stella makes many things with oysters, from Oysters Rockefeller, to po'boys, to stuffing for smoked turkey breasts. What I love for her to make is her oyster chowder. With French bread and lots of butter, I indulge myself and deliberately make several loud slurps, driving Jennie crazy under the table.

Normally, for fish we rely on what Stella or our friends catch. Since it is literally catch as catch can, the recipes for cooking them need to be very versatile. There are all kinds of fish and they can be cooked in a number of ways.

Grilling fillets is a nice quick way to have them with French bread for a lunch. But poached with a simple hollandaise sauce and some small potatoes and peas makes a nice meal. Then there is the increasingly popular blackened style.

For a large party we turn to the markets for redfish for Stella to make Baked Redfish Courtbouillon, augmenting it with some smoked turkey breast or ham. She starts these meals with Oysters Bienville ala Stella, modifying the standard Oysters Bienville recipe by boiling the shrimp in her own selection of spices.

We recently had a party for about forty people who were in town for a meeting I was helping host. Stella wanted to serve them Trout Amandine. To get it to them in a "just off the skillet" condition, she had me cook them in oil in the smaller of the two pots that go with our turkey fryer (a unit with large pots that sit on low gas units).

When the oil reached the right temperature, I dropped in about six or so fish. These cooked very quickly and were hustled inside. There, Stella placed them on plates with vegetables and served them to guests, while I cooked up another half dozen.

Most of the preparation for the meal took place before the guests arrived. The actual cooking and serving while they were here took less than twenty-five minutes. Not a bad nights work and we had the time to enjoy the company of our guests.

*... PAUL*

# *MY FISH AND SEAFOOD RECIPES*

*W*e live in a maritime community and so our diet is heavily involved in the seafood caught locally in the Sound or Gulf. As a result, the recipes in this chapter dip a little into that seafood. Not, perhaps nearly enough. To do it justice would take a book by itself. But I think this sampling is a pretty good representation.

However, let me take a few minutes to give a few tips on seafood in general that may be helpful. The first tip is that for truly fresh fish; catch your own! If you can't do that, then find a good seafood dealer (market or boat) that you find over time is reliable and stick with them.

Know what you are buying and what to look for to insure that your seafood is fresh. This takes a bit of experience. Let's talk about how to tell if the fish you are presented is fresh. The best indicator is smell. There should be no "fishy" smell and there should be no questions asked when you ask to smell the fish.

Then look at the whole fish. The fish should have eyes that are clear and not caved in or milky in color. Touch the fish. The flesh should spring back when pressed lightly with your finger. A fish that fails any one of these tests should be rejected.

Finally, buy whole fish - fillets are usually an indication of some age on the fish and that the proprietor is trying to salvage an aging catch. (Fresh frozen is the exception to this, however).

Shrimp should be purchased with their heads on. This is a pretty sure indicator that they have been recently caught. On the other hand, you should also know that freshly caught shrimp are difficult to peel and need to sit on some ice for a couple of hours before you start cleaning them. Also, please remember that even if you put them in the refrigerator, keep them on ice anyway. This goes for all your seafood.

The shrimp should have no discoloration to their shells. For instance, there should be no slight pink to the shells. This is an indicator of shrimp that are past their prime. And, of course, smell is again a good clue.

I like to buy crabs that are alive - no exceptions. Packed crabmeat should be checked for the expiration date and that good old standby of smell is still your best indicator. The same rule applies to shucked oysters.

I don't really have any good guidelines for oysters in the shell, except using a reputable dealer.

If you happen to use clams or mussels, make sure that their shells close tightly when they are touched. If the shell remains open, the occupant has passed on to clam or mussel heaven and you will wish you could too, if you cook and eat one of them.

The chapter involves several different ways to cook seafood. One way that has received a great deal of attention the last few years is "blackening" and I have added a recipe for blackening fish in this chapter. Let me emphasize that blackening is just another way to cook, like poaching or grilling or frying. Each method lends itself to cooking a fish (or a meat or a poultry) in a particular way. Explore this method. It's different, but I think you will like the results.

One last bit of advice. Remember that you get what you pay for. There are no "deals" on good fresh seafood. The people who bring us these wonderful delights work hard for their living and they deserve fair pay for their efforts.

*... STELLA*

## BAKED REDFISH COURTBOUILLON

| | |
|---|---|
| 4 slices bacon | 2 cloves |
| 3 tbsp. butter | ½ tsp. each thyme, salt |
| 2 large onions |    and pepper |
| 1 clove garlic | 5 lb redfish |
| 3 cups cooked or canned tomatoes | Sliced hard cooked eggs, |
| 1 bay leaf |    black olives |

Fry bacon until crisp. Drain on paper towel, crumble and set aside. Add butter to bacon fat. Chop onions and garlic and then sauté in butter and bacon fat until tender. Rub tomatoes through a sieve or put through a food mill and add to onions and garlic. Add bay leaf, cloves, thyme, salt and pepper. Simmer for 30 minutes.

Leaving head and tail intact, clean redfish by scaling and washing. Pat dry. Salt and pepper interior of fish and place in oiled baking pan. Pour sauce over fish and bake in 425-degree oven for 25 minutes, or until fish flakes easily when tested with fork. Baste often while cooking.

Remove fish to a hot presentation platter. Pour sauce around it. Garnish with sliced eggs and black olives. Sprinkle crumpled bacon over fish. If sauce seems thick, dilute with red wine.

 *Serve with saffron rice, garlic bread and mixed green salad dressed with a good vinegar and oil dressing.*

 *Baked Redfish makes a good presentation at a dinner party, so take advantage of this when you decide to do this recipe. And if the party is for a special person, remember that that person gets to eat the cheeks!*

\*\*\*\*\*

## TROUT AMANDINE ala Stella

### Fish Preparation

| | |
|---|---|
| 4 trout fillets | Salt and pepper to taste |
| 1 cup milk | Cayenne pepper |
| Flour | |

### Amandine Sauce

| | |
|---|---|
| ½ lb. butter | 2 tbsp. lemon juice |
| 3/4 cup slivered almonds | Dash of Worcestershire sauce |
| 1 tsp. ground black pepper | |

Wash trout fillets and pat dry. Place in a shallow baking dish, cover with milk, and marinate at least 30 minutes or, if possible, overnight. Drain fillets and dust with flour seasoned with salt, pepper and a little cayenne pepper. Set aside.

In a skillet, prepare sauce. Melt ¼ lb. butter and add almonds. Brown almonds very slowly until they become toasted to a medium brown color. Add freshly ground black pepper, lemon juice, and Worcestershire sauce. Cook an additional minute.

In a separate skillet, melt the remaining butter and add small amount of olive oil. Continue heating until hot enough to sauté. Sauté fish until golden brown on each side. Remove to serving dish and place almonds and sauce over fish.

Serve immediately. Serves four as the main course.

 *It is extremely important to serve the fish hot. Adding the olive oil to the butter allows you to bring the temperature high enough to sauté the trout without burning the butter.*

 *Do not overcook the trout! This will destroy their delicate flavor. Remember that we are adding this delicious sauce to emphasize the trout flavor. If that flavor is gone, we have lost the reason for making the recipe to begin with.*

*****

# CRABMEAT QUICHE

½ cup mayonnaise
2 tbsp. flour
2 eggs, beaten
½ cup milk
12 oz. crabmeat

8 oz. Swiss cheese, shredded
1/3 cup green onion, chopped
¼ cup green pepper, diced
6 fresh white mushrooms, sliced
4 strips cooked bacon, crumbled

Mix together mayonnaise, flour, eggs and milk. Add crabmeat, Swiss cheese, onion, pepper, mushrooms and bacon. Put in a pastry shell and bake at 350 degrees for 40 - 45 minutes.

Serve immediately. Serves six.

 *This is very good dish that can be served either hot, at room temperature, or cold. As a matter of fact, it is really good lukewarm the next day when the flavors have had time to meld. It also makes a nice breakfast dish to have on the sideboard on weekends for late sleeping guests.*

**\*\*\*\*\***

## FRESH TUNA STEAK in a Garden

| | |
|---|---|
| 1 tbsp. olive oil | 1 med. tomato |
| 1 clove garlic | 1 med. green pepper |
| 1 lb. fresh tuna steak | 1 med. cucumber |
| Salt, pepper, and thyme | 1 small sweet onion |
| 1 small head Romaine lettuce | Balsamic vinegar |

Heat tablespoon olive oil in skillet, adding garlic clove sliced in two. Brown garlic lightly and remove from skillet. Add tuna steaks seasoning each with salt, pepper and thyme. Cook three minutes on each side or until steaks are pink on inside. After steaks are cooked, put them aside to cool.

While steaks are cooling, prepare salad base starting with lettuce that has been broken into bite-sized pieces. Slice and add the remaining vegetables to lettuce. Make sure all have been chilled.

Separate tuna steaks into large flakes and place on top of the salad base. Dress with olive oil and balsamic vinegar. Serve with French bread or rolls.

Serves two as a main course.

*Do Not Overcook The Tuna! If you do, the wonderful taste of the tuna will completely disappear. This makes an excellent summer meal for either lunch or supper and can be quite filling. You can get creative and add any number of salad-type articles to the recipe, i.e., boiled eggs, artichokes, celery, etc.*

\*\*\*\*\*

# BLACKENED "ANY FISH"

### Seasoning Mix

| | |
|---|---|
| 1 tbsp. sweet paprika | 1 tsp. cayenne pepper |
| 2 tsp. salt | ¾ tsp. white pepper |
| 1 tsp. garlic powder | ¾ tsp. black pepper |
| 1 tsp. onion powder | ½ tsp. ground thyme |

Thoroughly mix all ingredients of seasoning mix together and set aside.

### Fish

**4 fish fillets (must be a firm fish such as redfish, tuna, pompano)**
**1 cup melted unsalted butter**

Wash the fillets and pat dry. Liberally rub seasoning into fillet. Dip each fillet in butter and place them side by side in a flat pan. Place in refrigerator and chill for at least one hour.

Set grill on high temperature and place cast iron skillet on grill to heat. Skillet should heat until there appears to be a white ash on bottom. This is extremely important. This is an indicator of the skillet being hot enough to do the blackening of your fish. Bring out fish and place in skillet. Cook about 2 minutes on each side.

Serve immediately while hot. Drizzle a little additional melted butter on each fillets along with a few drops of freshly squeezed lemon juice.

  *This is best done on an outside gas grill and the description given above is for cooking on one of those units. This brings up an important point about outside grills. Charcoal grills are nice for occasional picnics, but for backyard grilling, use a gas grill. It's simpler to use and you can get a hotter grill quicker with more control of the heat.*

 *The seasoning combined with the high temperature is the key to any blackened recipe. When the fish is placed on the skillet, the blackening of the outside flesh seals the juices inside the fish and, as the juices boil, the seasoning permeates the entire fish.*

*The seasoning mix can be adjusted to accommodate your own personal preferences; add or eliminate any of my seasoning to suit your taste. I make my seasoning mix in quantity and place it in a tightly sealed container in the freezer so it doesn't lose its flavor.*

*Be absolutely sure to start with the freshest possible seasonings. This is very important and overlooked by a lot of cooks. A few years ago, I started to notice a loss in flavor with some of my recipes. When I checked, I found that several of my seasonings had become flat due to age. Since then, I date my spices when I purchase them. If possible spices should be kept in a cool dark place to help prolong their lives.*

*This blackening recipe is very versatile and can be used on any number of other items such as steak, pork chops or chicken; all cooked in the same "blackened" manner. Again, the seasoning and hot grill are the key factors. Adjust your seasoning to fit what kind of meat or poultry you are cooking.*

**\*\*\*\*\***

## STUFFED FLOUNDER

1 med. sized onion, finely minced
8 tbsp. butter (no substitutes)
1 stalk celery, finely chopped
¼ green pepper, finely chopped
¾ lb. boiled crabmeat
Pinch of thyme
½ cup of coarse chopped pecans

1 small bay leaf
1 tsp. Worcestershire sauce
½ cup cream
Breadcrumbs
Salt and pepper
4 small flounder
2 tbsp. cooking oil
3 oz. sherry or white wine
½ fresh lemon, juice of

Sauté onions in 4 tablespoon of butter until soft and brown. Add celery and pepper and sauté for 2 to 3 minutes more. Add crabmeat, thyme, coarsely chopped pecans, bay leaf, Worcestershire sauce, cream and enough breadcrumbs to hold mixture together or to stretch amount of dressing needed. Add salt and pepper and stuff fish.

Place cooking oil and 2 tablespoons butter in a broiler pan and add fish. Broil slowly under low flame, periodically basting with pan juices. Add sherry or wine to produce more juices and help flavor fish. When fish are golden brown or slightly darker on top, they are cooked.

Serve on individual plates and spoon sauce over fish. Sprinkle with lemon juice. Serves four.

*I completely debone my flounder before I do the stuffing. This makes the stuffing process much easier. Also, it's a consideration for your guests as they won't have to worry about having to separate the bones when eating your nicely cooked fish. They'll thank you for it.*

*Remember, flounder is a very dry fish, so please use butter in the cooking process. DO NOT USE A SUBSTITUTE. Also, this is a very, very rich dish and should be served with rather simple accompaniments. Try serving with a fresh green salad, some fresh garden peas, and crusty warm French bread. All of these will compliment the fish quite nicely.*

\*\*\*\*\*

## *FRIED SOFT-SHELL CRABS*

**4 soft-shell crabs**       **Baking powder**
**1 cup milk**               **Brown paper bag**
**Salt and pepper**          **Butter**
**Dash of Tabasco**          **Few drops of olive oil**
**Flour**                    **Lemon juice and/or tartar sauce**

Clean crabs by rinsing thoroughly and removing the lungs (dead fingers) and entrails in the center of the crab.  Cut off eyes and mouth. Soak crabs in the milk, salt and pepper and Tabasco for at least one hour - the longer the better.  Put flour and a few pinches of baking powder in a brown paper bag and shake crabs in the flour mixture very gently, one at a time.

Heat butter in heavy skillet until melted, adding a few drops of olive oil so the butter doesn't burn.  Gently sauté crabs until golden brown. Remove from skillet and drain on paper towels.  Season immediately.

Serve with a few squeezes of lemon juice and / or tartar sauce. Serves four.

 *This crab dish and the flavor of many fish dishes are enhanced by tartar sauce. Use the tartar sauce  recipe at the end of this chapter to make your own.*

*****

## STEAMED CRABS (Eastern Shore Style)

| | |
|---|---|
| 1 qt. water | 1 small box Old Bay seasoning |
| 2 dozen live blue crabs | 1 qt. beer |
| 2 cups salt | |

Place insert in large steaming or canning pot and add water. Bring
water to boil. Place one layer of crabs atop insert. Put lid on pot (the
heat will usually calm the crabs down). Remove lid and sprinkle crabs
liberally with salt and some Old Bay Seasonings. Put in another layer
of crabs, cover with lid, uncover and sprinkle salt and Old Bay.
Continue layering in this fashion until all the crabs and seasoning are
in pot. Add beer, cover and steam for 20 minutes. Remove crabs and
serve on a large tray on an outside table covered with newspaper or
butcher paper.

Serve with separate bowls of pure vinegar and a combination of drawn
butter and lemon juice. You can also make a dry mixture of salt and
Old Bay for dipping.

*Steaming rather than boiling the crabs helps them retain more
of their fat. The salt and the seasoning adhere to the crabs and
this adds to their general flavor as you crack and pick each
crab.*

*Some people like vinegar with their crabs, others like drawn
butter and lemon juice. The vinegar enhances the already
sweet taste of the crabmeat, while the butter and lemon juice
just makes everything taste better.*

*****

# CRAB CAKES

| | |
|---|---|
| 1  lb. fresh crabmeat | ¾  cup crushed cornflakes |
| 1  egg, slightly beaten | Salt and freshly ground pepper |
| 1  tsp. prepared mustard | 1/8 to 1/4 lb. butter |
| 1½  tsp. mayonnaise | |

If you can, catch your own crabs. These always taste better for some reason. Cook crabs by steaming or boiling and then pick and remove all shells from crabmeat.  Add egg, mustard, mayonnaise, cornflakes, salt and ground pepper. Mix gently with your hands. Divide mixture into six patty portions to form cakes.  Cover and chill cakes for about 1 hour to allow flavors to blend.

Melt butter in a large skillet over medium heat.  Place crab cakes in skillet and brown on both sides. Serve immediately. May be served on beds of lettuce with fresh cuts of tomato on the side. Include on the side, mayonnaise, tarter sauce, and Tabasco.

Serves 6.

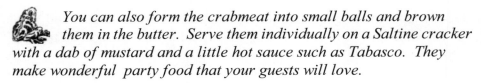 *You can also form the crabmeat into small balls and brown them in the butter.  Serve them individually on a Saltine cracker with a dab of mustard and a little hot sauce such as Tabasco.  They make wonderful  party food that your guests will love.*

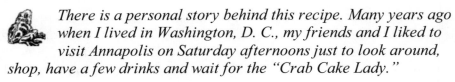 *There is a personal story behind this recipe. Many years ago when I lived in Washington, D. C., my friends and I liked to visit Annapolis on Saturday afternoons just to look around, shop, have a few drinks and wait for the "Crab Cake Lady."*

*She made wonderful little crab cakes that she sandwiched between two Saltine crackers and dressed with mustard and hot sauce.  She walked the streets of  downtown Annapolis selling her crab cakes on Saturday afternoons for 25 cents apiece.*

*Our big accomplishment on these Saturdays was to be get to the crab lady first to get the crab cakes before they were all gone. This was harder than it sounds as you never knew where she would start her trip on any particular Saturday. So it was a big game for us to see who could find her first and get some of her wonderful crab cakes.*

*She was kind enough to give me the gist of her recipe. I've tried to reconstruct it here as best I can.*

\*\*\*\*\*

## TARTAR SAUCE

**½ small onion, finely minced**
**½ to ¾ cup mayonnaise**
**2 to 3 tsp. capers**
**2 to 3 sweet pickles, finely chopped**

**Parsley, fresh**
**1 tbsp. lemon juice**
**Sugar**

Gently mix onions, mayonnaise, capers, pickles, fresh parsley and lemon juice together. Add dash of sugar and taste. Refrigerate for about 2 hours to allow flavors to combine.

*The sugar should be used sparingly. It is only there to cut the acidity of the other ingredients. You will have to experiment to get the mixture you like best. The combination of the capers and the fresh parsley really enhances this sauce as well as the seafood it is to accompany. If you really want to step this up, make your own mayonnaise.*

\*\*\*\*\*

# *MEAT AND POULTRY*

**MARIO y PAOLA ROAST CHICKEN**
**STEAK DIANE**
**PEPPER STEAK**
**LAMB CHOPS**
**"BUTTERFLY" LEG OF LAMB**

# MARIO y PAOLA

During the several years my work required extensive foreign traveling, I tried to take Stella with me on at least one trip a year to ease the pressure my absence made to our marriage. On one trip to La Spezia, Italy, she couldn't come with me and I had to go alone.

After spending several days getting the things done that I needed to do in the city, I went with some close friends, Paola and Mario, to their weekend place in the hills 40 miles east of the city.

I had been there before and during that visit I had had Stella with me. So, I looked forward to my weekend. When we arrived, I found that it was as I remembered it, a wonderful retreat, removed from all the things that I was normally accustomed to in my everyday life. The involved work that I had been engaged in that past week seemed to have occurred in some other time, and I started to truly relax.

My room that night was the upper floor of a small stone house a thousand years old. I slept on a straw mattress and was warmed by a fire in the small raised fireplace by the bed. I fell asleep watching the firelight flicker on the stone walls of my small room. Later that night, I awoke and listened to the night noises around me. Outside my window, I could hear a waterfall and a bird that sang to me and the rest of the world through most of the night.

The next morning we had an Italian breakfast of coffee, toast and a piece of fruit and went to the rear of the house to look at my friend Mario's small vineyard. He proudly showed me his rows of grapes and assured me that if I came back the next fall we would make wine using the old wine press under the village church (I actually did go back and we did make wine that year. It was very good).

At midday we went to the local restaurante / bar and sat in a room with the locals from the tiny village for our Sunday meal. The room held only a few large tables; no real menu. People sat wherever there was room and were served by large plates of food that continuously came out of the kitchen.

Through the windows, I could see the valley and hills and a small village on the hill to our right. I knew it was going to be a long meal and relaxed in the ambiance of good food and wonderful people.

Paola, Mario's wife was upset that Stella had not been able to make the trip with me.

She said so to me and also to the people that joined us at our table, and to the restaurante proprietor at the bar as well as the cook in the kitchen (who had learned her English in Scotland and spoke it with a rich Scottish burr).

I sat explaining why Stella wasn't with me for perhaps the tenth time when I heard Paola's voice over the noise in the room, "Stella! How are you?" I looked up to see Paola on the phone in the corner of the room. She had called Stella in Mississippi!!

I quickly got up to go talk to her myself, when someone stopped me to say hello. When I looked again, the proprietor had started to talk to Stella explaining something about the menu, then the cook came on to clarify what he had said, then someone I knew couldn't speak English, started singing her an Italian song.

It seemed everyone in the room got to talk to Stella before I did that day.

Later when I returned home, Stella told me about having the wonderful experience of going to bed in Mississippi and waking to the phone ringing and finding herself for a little over a half hour in a small village in the northern hills of Italy.

### ... PAUL

# MY MEAT AND POULTRY RECIPES

*A*lthough I missed the trip Paul speaks about, I have been with him on other occasions to visit Italy and over the years we have spent some very memorable weeks in both Naples in the south and La Spezia in the north.

*From a food standpoint, my visits were remarkable. I learned why Italian cuisine is considered one of the finest in the world. There is a style and approach to their eating that is unique and one I have remembered and try to instill in my cooking. I found southern Italian food was fantastic and so was northern Italian, but I also found both were much different in style and taste.*

*Where but in Naples would you walk by your customary restaurant and have the head waiter come rushing out and ask what time you would be eating there that night?*

*It seems that he had an exceptionally nice fish that he wanted us to try, but since it took a while to fix, the chef needed to know when we would be eating. I told him and that night Paul and I and a friend had a remarkable meal. Yet when I mentioned what had happened to our Neapolitan friends, they thought it quite normal.*

*What was different about our visits with Mario and Paola was that unlike other Europeans who, when they have visitors, consider their town or city their dining room and take you out to eat, Mario and Paola often entertain their guests with diners at their home. And wonderful dinners these were.*

*From this I was able to get in the kitchen and witness a completely different way of cooking than what I have been accustomed to. I've added Mario and Paola's chicken recipe as the first of the dishes in this chapter. It is a very nice dish. Try it. I think you will enjoy it.*

As to the meat section of this chapter, I have found that most meat dishes are best enjoyed when the meat is cooked so as to be able to stand alone on its own merits.

Take steak for example. Why add Worcestershire sauce to a perfectly delicious steak? If your steak needs this strong type of flavor reinforcement, you have bought a poor cut of steak. Try another butcher.

This is an important point to remember and is basic to all of my cooking, not just meat. The entrée of a meal should be allowed to stand on its own. I would be the first to admit that sauces are nice with any dish, whether poultry, meat or fish. In fact a good sauce is a delight and a pleasure that can bring a dish to its true height of flavor. But I believe that on most occasions, a good sauce should be to used to enhance the flavor of the entrée not to hide a poor cut of meat.

There are exceptions, of course, certainly barbequed pork, chicken and beef being good examples, and there are others. But to me a good rule of thumb to follow whether with fish, meat or fowl is to let whatever it is you are cooking be allowed to be itself.

## An Important Note on Cooking Chicken.

All poultry is prone to salmonella. You need to be particularly careful when cooking or handling raw chicken. Wash your hands thoroughly and clean your utensils and cutting board in the dishwasher after dealing with chicken. Under no circumstances should you proceed with the rest of the meal without making sure everything has been thoroughly cleaned!

*... STELLA*

## MARIO y PAOLA ROAST CHICKEN

| | |
|---|---|
| 1  roasting hen | 1 cup olives (marinated  in olive |
| salt and pepper | oil and vinegar) |
| 4 cloves garlic, peeled | ¼ cup melted butter |
| 4 sprigs fresh rosemary | |

Carefully wash and clean chicken and pat dry.  Season inside of chicken with salt and pepper and place it in roasting pan with breast side up.  Crush garlic with the blade of your chef's knife and place two cloves in the cavity of the chicken along with two sprigs of rosemary and 5 or 6 olives.  The remaining garlic, rosemary and olives should be placed in the bottom of the roasting pan.

Roast chicken at 350 degrees for 45 minutes or until the juices run clear.  Uncover chicken and roast for an additional 15 minutes until chicken browns nicely.  Baste chicken often through roasting process with melted butter and juices from the pan.

Remove from oven and let sit for about 10 minutes and serve. Excellent when served with long grain and wild rice, candied carrots, and a cucumber salad.

*I have tried to recreate this from memory; a memory of a wonderful Sunday afternoon dinner prepared for us by Mario and Paola.  While the chicken I make is very good, it never seems to equal the efforts of Mario and Paola.  I think the secret to their success is that they use olives harvested from their own trees that are marinated in their own special seasoning.*

*****

### STEAK DIANE

#### Steaks

4 ½ lb. steaks ½" thick (top loin, strip, rib-eye or Delmonico
1 ½ tbsp. freshly ground black pepper

Soy sauce (few drops)
Olive oil
2 tbsp. butter

#### Sauce

4 tbsp. butter
¼ cup minced shallots and parsley
Mixture of 1 tbsp. cornstarch, fresh parsley, 1 tbsp. Dijon mustard and 1 cup of bouillon

Worcestershire sauce
½ fresh lemon, juice of
Cognac or Port

Trim steaks of all fat and gristle. Pound between two pieces of wax paper or in a strong plastic bag to ¼" thickness. Rub pepper into one side of each steak and add few drops of soy sauce and olive oil. Turn and repeat on other sides. Place on a platter and refrigerate until ready to cook.

Preheat skillet to a hot temperature and add some olive oil and 2 teaspoons butter. Sauté two steaks at a time for 30 to 40 seconds, turn immediately and repeat. Roll steaks up and place on a platter on the side.

Add more butter to skillet and let mixture foam up. Add shallots and parsley and cook for a moment. Add mixture of cornstarch, parsley, mustard, and bouillon. Stir briefly and then add a few drops of Worcestershire sauce, the lemon juice and liquor.

Unroll steaks in sauce and spoon sauce over steak to help even the distribution of sauce flavor in meat. Cook other steaks in same fashion.

Serve immediately. Serves 4.

*****

## PEPPER STEAK

1 lb. flank steak, partially
frozen
½ cup soy sauce
2 tbsp. light olive oil
1 clove garlic, sliced in two

1 large green pepper, sliced in
½" strips
1 large tomato, cut in ½" sections
1 tsp. cornstarch

Freeze flank steak until partially frozen so that it can be easily sliced. Cut into almost paper thin slices and marinate in ¼ cup soy sauce for an hour. Using a wok or shallow skillet, heat olive oil until hot. Add garlic and cook until it browns slightly. Remove garlic particles from oil. Add peppers and stir-fry for two minutes or until their skin begins to blister. Add tomatoes and cook an additional two minutes, stirring constantly.

Add steak and cook for an additional two to three minutes until steak is barely cooked. Make a mixture of remaining of soy sauce and cornstarch and add to steak and vegetables. Stir until mixture just begins to thicken.

Remove from heat and serve over bed of hot white rice.

*The garlic gives a surprisingly subtle taste to the dish. Remember to have all your ingredients ready before you start cooking as this is a stir-fry dish and the actual cooking occurs rapidly. This keeps well refrigerated for up to three days and is a great left over.*

\*\*\*\*\*

## LAMB CHOPS

**Olive oil**
**8 lamb chops, 1 inch thick**
**Salt, pepper, garlic powder and rosemary**

Heat a heavy skillet to medium heat and add a tablespoon of olive oil. Turn heat up to high and let oil heat up. Add chops one at a time and season with salt, pepper, garlic powder and rosemary. Sear chops and cook on each side for three minutes.

Serve immediately. Serve with mint jelly, seasoned rice and candied carrots. Serves 4.

 *Searing the chops, or just about any other meat, will help retain their natural juices inside the chops (This is in fact very much like the blackening process described in the fish chapter).*

 *The chops can also be grilled on your outside grill. This brings up a point about outside grills. Charcoal is nice for picnics, but for serious backyard grilling, use a gas grill. It's simpler to use and there is no difference in flavor. In this case, the average charcoal would not give you the reliable heat needed to effectively seal the natural juices inside the meat.*

 *This makes a great "company" dinner and you will impress your guests. Especially if the chops are done on the outside gas grill.*

*It seems the hocus pocus macho-ness of seeing Paul working on the relatively simple job of cooking the chops on the gas grill is more impressive to guests than seeing me do the same thing on the kitchen stove. I don't care. It gets the guests, the heat, and part of the cooking out of my kitchen, allowing me to worry over the candied carrots, rice and the salad.*

*****

## "BUTTERFLY" LEG OF LAMB

1 leg of lamb
2 large cloves garlic
½ tsp. salt
2 tbsp. Dijon-style mustard
1 tbsp. soy sauce

1 ½ teaspoons ground rosemary, thyme or oregano
2 tbsp. freshly squeezed lemon juice
¼ cup olive oil or butter

Get your butcher to butterfly the leg of lamb. Make a marinade of the next seven ingredients and marinate the lamb over night. Cook on low to medium setting on barbeque grill while basting throughout the process with any remaining marinade, olive oil or melted butter with a little lemon juice.

Lamb is done when it gets a springy texture to the pressure of your fingers. Internal temperature should be between 120 and 130 degrees to get a rare or medium rare finish.

Remove lamb from oven and let it rest for 15 to 20 minutes. Remember that it will be still cooking during this cooling period, so watch you don't overcook it initially.

Thinly slice and serve. Serve with rice and salad.

 *While you prepare other ingredients for your meal, you can keep the lamb warm for a good hour by placing it in a 120 degree oven.*

\*\*\*\*\*

# SIDE DISHES

*CANDIED CARROTS*
*BARBEQUE VEGETABLES*
*POTATOES WHISPERING PINES*
*DOLCE ACORN SQUASH*
*FRIED CABBAGE*

# *LET'S TALK*

*"The table was made for conversation. Bring on the food and let's talk."*

*Willey Murke, 1903*

Several years ago I spent some time at the University of Liege in Belgium. I had been there before and found it a nice place to visit. So, when I had a chance to make an extended stay, I took it.

It's their food that I really enjoy. There is, of course, the normal European cuisine and amenities. For example, while Stella was fixing our eggs for breakfast, I would run downstairs and get fresh, still warm from the oven bread from the baker a few feet from our door. And later in the day, she would go out and buy fresh local produce and other ingredients for that night's supper.

But there is more to their food than the typical European atmosphere and fare. Their food is different. It took me a little while to get used to the differences, but once I did I was delighted. It was gourmet food with flair.

Imagine roast gooseneck! Whole squab in aspic! My friends took pleasure in taking me to places that would leave me wondering what it was I had eaten. So, I was puzzled when two close friends took me on a farewell outing to a place they said served steak.

Just getting there was an adventure. We retraced our path several time, each of my two friends claiming the other had given wrong directions. But once there, it was worth the trouble. The food was, as usual, different. And that difference was delightful.

The restaurant specialized in a main entrée that were exceptional cuts of seasoned aged prime beef. These were cooked a piece at a time on a hot book-sized stone that was placed in front of each of us. How the stone retained its heat during the meal was beyond me, but it did.

**70**

As we sat and talked, I noticed an elderly couple near us. The man was heavy set and sat stolidly addressing his meat, cutting long thin slivers and placing them on the stone. When the meat was seared to his satisfaction, he would place it carefully in his mouth. Once there, he chewed each piece in an almost reflective manner, before leaning forward and cutting another piece.

His small wife sat opposite him with a dour look that seemed to encompass her whole being. Her eating mannerism was distinctly different from his. She addressed her food with a chicken-like stare, then cutting several small chunks, cooked each thoroughly to a near-burn. Then she placed each in her mouth where it disappeared without any show of taste or pleasure. There would be a long pause, as if waiting for some inner trapdoor to close, and then she would start anew.

What was particularly unusual was that throughout their meal there was no conversation! None! He meditatively sliced and munched; she looked, diced and swallowed. All without one word between them. Did the man and his wife know one another so well that they had nothing more to say to each other? Or that each knew what the other was thinking and nothing needed to be said.

The two had been there when we came in and we were well into our meal when I realized they were leaving. He walked ponderously ahead of her, a ship in the roads; passing the tables as if they were marker buoys. The woman, moving like a small sparrow, scurried after him.

I watched them for a brief moment as they departed and then was drawn back into the spirited conversation of my friends and a wonderfully, delightful meal. Friends, good friends, leave great memories and when good friend are combined with good food, great meals become superb meals.

Last year I took Stella out to dinner on our twenty-fifth wedding anniversary. We went to a small restaurant a block off the water in downtown Gulfport. Our conversation during the meal ranged over many things. What did we talk about? I don't remember, but we did enjoy ourselves.

I look forward to the meal we have together at the end of the next twenty-five years. A lot of things will have happened and we'll have a great deal to talk about.

*... PAUL*

71

# *MY SIDE DISH RECIPES*

*T*o *be truthful, for most of our meals we have very simple side dishes.*

*Normally, these are either rice or potatoes accompanied by a salad such as I've described in the "Appetizer and Salad" chapter. I usually fix the rice and potatoes in different ways for variety, but basically these ways are extremely basic preparations.*

*If I do fix a dish besides potatoes or rice, it's still one that doesn't take much preparation. Sweet corn is a good example.*

*Paul and I both love when "Silver Queen" comes into season and I can get up early on a Saturday morning and get a dozen ears at the Hancock County Farmers' market for that night's supper.*

*If you want them to have that fresh "just picked that morning," Silver Queen flavor, don't even think about buying them at the super market. Even when you buy them at the farmers' market, know your vendors. Some are much more reliable as to the freshness of what they sell than others.*

*For dinner that evening (and it has to be the same day to get the full flavor of the corn), I boil them and serve them with the entrée with room temperature butter and salt and ground pepper. We have a big plate for the spent ears and it fills rapidly.*

*For variation, I sometimes slice the kernels off the cob and fry them in a pan with just butter, salt, pepper and garlic. Serve with French bread, a simple green salad and a tall glass of iced sun tea. This is simplicity itself and it is good.*

*Fresh green beans from my garden or various squashes are other examples and there are many other fresh vegetables that can be fixed just as quickly and easily.*

*For example, I steam the green beans till they are slightly tender and serve them with butter, freshly ground pepper and salt. Or, if you don't want to use butter, squeeze a few drops of lemon juice on the vegetables. You will find the fresh lemon juice will sharply enhance their sweet, natural goodness and will markedly cut down on the calories involved.*

*What could be easier? All make delicious additions to a meal without a great deal of bother. My problem here is that all of these are so easy to fix, that it seems superfluous to write them down as recipes for another person to follow.*

*And yet as easy as they are to fix, they make up a good part of the side dishes we normally have with our meals. As a result, you will find the side dish recipes in this particular chapter are a little sparse. But remember that the ones I have included are good and worth your investigation.*

*Finally, let me make a point here that I have stated before.*

*I strongly suggest that although the side dishes are an adjunct to the overall flavor of the meal; don't treat any side dish as an added chore. As with my suggestion for the salad, take the time and care with it as you do with any other part of the meal.*

*... STELLA*

# CANDIED CARROTS

| | |
|---|---|
| 1 lb. fresh carrots | 3 tbsp. Water |
| 3 tbsp. butter | Salt and pepper |
| 3 tbsp. brown sugar | |

Clean carrots and slice.  Place in boiling water and cook until just barely tender.  Remove from heat and drain.  Return to pan and add butter, sugar and water.

Place on low heat until butter and sugar caramelize.  Season with salt and pepper.

Serve immediately.

Serves 4 to 6.

 *This side dish keeps well in the refrigerator for a few days and is a great leftover.*

*It also freezes very nicely. I'm a real big fan of making a large recipe and packaging it into several meal-size servings and freezing them.  But, in all truth, they really are so easy to make, that taking the few minutes to make it is not a real concern.*

**\*\*\*\*\***

## BARBEQUE VEGETABLES

| | |
|---|---|
| 1 large baking potato | 1 med.  zucchini squash |
| 3 carrots | 1 stick butter |
| 2 med. onions | Salt and pepper |
| 3 stalks celery | ½ tsp. Worcestershire sauce |
| 2 med. tomatoes | |

Cut vegetable into bite-size pieces and arrange in baking pan.  Season with salt and pepper and Worcestershire Sauce.  Melt butter and drizzle over vegetables.  Wrap in aluminum foil and place on grill.

Cook slowly until almost tender.  Remove foil and continue cooking until vegetables brown.

Serves 4 to 6.

 *This does nicely when served with a good roast or steak that has been grilled at the same time. While I believe it tastes best when cooked on an outside gas grill (don't ask me why), it can also be effectively cooked in the oven.*

*****

## POTATOES WHISPERING PINES

**2 lb. new red potatoes (small)**
**¼ lb. butter**
**½ tsp. garlic powder**
**Salt and pepper**

**2 tbsp. finely chopped fresh**
**parsley**
**6 tbsp. grated Parmesan or**
**Romano cheese (or both)**

Boil potatoes in their skins until tender.  Remove from pot and mash potatoes just enough to break their skin.  Add melted butter, garlic powder, salt, pepper and parsley and mix thoroughly.  Place mixture in a flat casserole dish and spread them over dish bottom.  Sprinkle cheese over potatoes.

Bake in a 375 degree oven for 30 minutes.  Check often so that they brown nicely, but do no burn.

Serve immediately. Serves 4 to 6.

 *This is both filling and a real crowd pleaser, especially with the "meat and potato" guys.*

\*\*\*\*\*

# DOLCE ACORN SQUASH

**2 acorn squash**
**4 tbsp. butter**
**4 tbsp. light brown sugar**

Cut squash in half and carefully cut a small slice across the rounded side of the squash so that it will sit flat on a plate. Removed seeds and membrane. Pierce each half of the squash with a fork making certain that it does not break outer skin of squash. Place butter and sugar in cavity.

Place in microwave and cook on high for approximately 5 minutes. Squash should be fork tender. Remove from microwave and let cool slightly before serving.

Serves four.

 *Note how easy it is to fix this dish! It makes a very nice side dish with grilled ham and is an excellent substitute for sweet potatoes. It keeps well as a left over, requiring only reheating.*

**\*\*\*\*\***

# FRIED CABBAGE

| | |
|---|---|
| ¼ cup butter | Salt and pepper |
| ½ cup chopped onion | 1 tsp. caraway seed |
| 4 cups chopped green cabbage | Apple cider vinegar |

Melt butter in large skillet.  Add onions and sauté until translucent.
Add cabbage and sauté for 5 minutes or until tender, but still crisp.
Season with salt and pepper and add caraway seeds.  Toss lightly and
sprinkle with about a tablespoon of vinegar.  Serve immediately.

Serves four.

 *This makes a very easy side dish to fix but it is good. It can be dressed up to look a little more elegant with a tablespoon or two of sour cream.*

*****

# *PASTAS*

*STELLA'S ALL PURPOSE TOMATO SAUCE*
*CHEESE RAVIOLI*
*GRANDMA'S EGG NOODLES*
*GRANDMA'S NOODLES AND CABBAGE*
*OYSTERS AND BRIE WITH PASTA*
*SHRIMP AND MUSHROOMS WITH PASTA*

# *"IT TAKES ABOUT FIFTEEN ROBINS TO MAKE A GOOD PIE."*

*Sing a song of sixpence, a pocket full of rye;*
*Four and twenty blackbirds, baked in a pie.*
*When the pie was opened ,the birds began to sing;*
*Wasn't that a dainty dish, to set before the king?*

The brick masons came by yesterday to fix a low brick wall behind the house. I knew the men. So I stayed and caught up on what had happened since I had last seen them. It was a father and son team, Joel and Joel, Jr. Both loved hunting and their talk was filled with hunting.

"Joel, he's been taking too much time off with hunting. Now he's got to hustle a bit to help pay for that new truck." The younger Joel pried an old Chicago brick from the offending wall. "Well, I tell ya," he said. "We had one of them deer steaks last night for supper and it sure were good eating."

As they talked, I remembered Stella and my trip with a friend up one of the bayous back of the Bay and the large flocks of robins we had seen. We were used to seeing at most two robins at a time and here there were hundreds swarming about the marsh bushes. We were also surprised when our friend told us that people used to hunt and eat robins.

"Tell me, Mr. Joel," I asked. "When you were young, did your mother ever bake you a pot pie filled with robins?"

"Why heck, yes. Now that's good eating. I loved it! It's all dark meat, kind of tangy, but real good. Oh my yes, it were good."

"How'd you get the robins?" "We'd shoot them with a pellet gun. We couldn't use 22's. Too much noise. The whole flock would take off. My mom sent me out to get some the first time when I was about eleven. We went out to the woods where they were swarming around some bushes and just picked them off one by one. My friend and I got about sixty each that day."

"Sixty! Did you need that many?" "Well yeah!" He laughed. "We just use the breasts! It takes about fifteen robins to make a good pot pie. My mother would make up several pies with what we got. We'd eat one and she'd put the rest up for eating later.

He stopped and gazed at the wall remembering and then bent forward and pried out another brick. "Yep, they sure were good eating. My mother would fix them together with some sort of dumplings and put a good thick crust of dough across the top and bake it. You could smell it cooking."

Stella had come up and, hearing what we were talking about, made a face. Joel laughed. "Why, Miss Stella, I bet you make Mr. Paul, here, some good chicken pot pies. Well I can't see much difference between robins and chicken except the price. People go hunting all the time. It's more than a sport with us, it's what we do, and it puts good food on the table. And I bet Mr. Paul likes a good steak, too"

Stella wasn't buying his argument and I realized that I had better change the conversation. "What about using squab in pot pies?"

"They're good, too. They don't taste the same, but they're good. When I was a kid, there was an old building complex over in Gulfport that were empty. Pigeons would nest there by the hundreds. We used to go there, climb up and get their squabs for pot pies. We didn't have to shoot them; just pick them out of the nest, throw them in a sack, and take them home to my mother to make into a pie. They didn't have no feathers so they were easy to fix up."

Stella now became interested and started asking questions about how they were cooked.

A few days later I saw a robin on the fence by the side of the house. I started to call Stella and ask her if she wanted to make a small pot pie for supper. Luckily, a wiser part of me made me keep the peace and I watched it hop about looking for berries and then, finally, fly away. As it flew away, I remembered something the brick mason had said when he left.

"There doesn't seem to be as many robins as there used to be."

## ... PAUL

# MY PASTA RECIPES

*P*astas make great dishes.

*A lot of people know this. It is no secret. Don't think of pastas as being only an Italian dish. For instance, stuffed pasta. The Italians have their ravioli, the Poles have their pierogi, and the Chinese have their wanton. I'm sure there are other examples equally as international.*

*Whatever they are called, I dearly love pastas. They're easy to fix, they're filling, they're remarkably healthy, they're simple to digest, they're economical as well as delicious and, best of all, they are fun.*

*When our grandchildren Lorelei and Michaela came for summer visits when they were younger, we used to make pasta in the kitchen on dry days. Paul would complain bitterly about having to dodge the pasta hanging out to dry around the room, but we noticed that he never hesitated to eat the finished product.*

*Pastas are good alone, with perhaps a little butter and a sprinkle of cheese. This is a wonderful way to fix them and is quick and simple. But there is a vast number of ways to fix them besides this that is also extremely easy and good.*

*But that is just the start. For even more versatility the word pasta actually covers an extremely large family that ranges from spaghettis to noodles. And all of the members of this large family offer exciting different dishes that can be cooked.*

*Paul and I like our rice and potatoes as side dishes to compliment a main entrée and sometimes we use pastas this way and they do very nicely. However, we believe all of these pastas are at their best when they become the main entrée itself. When this happens, they reach their full glory in both elegance and taste.*

*Blueberry Peaches, Red Robin Pie*

*Let me give you an example. Paul and I were down by the Waterside in Norfolk recently and mentioned to a waiter standing outside one of the restaurants that we on the Mississippi Gulf Coast can't easily get fresh mussels. We told him that we thought mussels cooked in their own juices with a pasta such as penne is a small bit of heaven.*

*He patiently listened to what we said, nodding sympathetically. Then he said he thought he could fix a dish like that for us and asked us to come inside; he would speak to the cook (it turned out he wasn't a waiter, but the owner of the restaurant).*

*He did and a little while later we were in a little bit of heaven eating a meal that could only be described as superb.*

*In this chapter I've only started to scratch the surface in presenting the great things that can be done with pasta. Unfortunately, to do so would take a book by itself. Please consider the recipes I've presented here as nice samples of a very wonderful food.*

*I hope you to enjoy this small sampling.*

*... STELLA*

## STELLA'S ALL PURPOSE TOMATO SAUCE

1 oz. dried Italian mushrooms
1 cup tepid water
3 tbsp. olive oil
2 large onions, finely chopped
2 cloves garlic, finely minced
2 med. sized carrots, finely shredded
2 cans (14 oz. each) beef broth

2 cans (1 lb. 14 oz. each) pear shaped tomatoes
1 tsp. each of salt, oregano leaves, rosemary leaves and sugar
2 tbsp. basil leaves
¼ tsp. pepper

Soak mushrooms in water for 5 minutes, drain, wash well (several washings) and chop. Set aside. Heat olive oil in a large Dutch oven over medium heat. Add onions, garlic and carrots and sauté for 5 minutes. Stir in mushrooms, beef broth, tomatoes (break them up with a fork), and seasonings. Boil gently for about 1 ½ hours until sauce is thick.

 *This is a great sauce with a hundred uses. It is a workhorse that can be called on again and again for use in a vast array of recipes. It makes a great basic sauce for lasagna, spaghetti, chicken and penne pasta, etc.*

 *I use it so much that I normally triple the recipe and freeze it in freezer bags in 2 cup sized portions. These stay frozen for long periods and are great to have when you just must have pasta as a side dish or the main entree. Defrost, and it's there ready to use.*

\*\*\*\*\*

# CHEESE RAVIOLI

### *Ravioli Dough*

**3 eggs**
**4 cups flour**
**¼ cup water**

Mix above until a dough is formed.  Knead until smooth and elastic.
Let rest before rolling out.

### *Ricotta Cheese Filling*

| | |
|---|---|
| **1 lb. Ricotta cheese** | **¾ cup grated Parmesan cheese** |
| **2 eggs** | **½ tbsp. salt** |
| **2 tbsp. finely chopped parsley** | **¼ tbsp. white pepper** |

Mix all ingredients until they are well incorporated.  Roll out dough on
a flat board.  Place about a teaspoon of filling about 2" apart on half the
dough. Fold the other half of the dough over the first half and seal.  Cut
evenly into squares to form the ravioli. Cook in boiling water until
squares float to the surface.  Do Not Overcook!

Drain and serve with sauce of choice or, as Paul likes it, just with
butter, salt, freshly ground pepper and a green salad.

Serves 4.

*****

## GRANDMA'S EGG NOODLES

| | |
|---|---|
| **1 cup all-purpose flour** | **¼ tsp. salt** |
| **1 large egg** | **1 tbsp. water** |

Mound flour on a board with a well in center. Drop in egg and salt. Beat in water with a fork. Bring flour into mixture until everything is completely incorporated. Knead resulting dough from center to outer edge until smooth. Roll out until very thin on a floured surface. Place dough on a floured cloth and let dry until it is no longer sticky, but not too brittle to handle. Sprinkle with flour and roll up tightly. Slice in thin strips and let dry for a couple of hours.

To cook, boil in salted water until noodles rise to the top. Drain and rinse in cold water and drain again.

\*\*\*\*\*

## GRANDMA'S NOODLES AND CABBAGE

| | |
|---|---|
| **¼ cup butter** | **½ tsp. salt** |
| **½ cup chopped onions** | **1/8 tsp. pepper** |
| **4 cup chopped/sliced cabbage** | **8 oz. egg noodles (wide cut)** |
| **1 tsp. caraway seeds** | **½ cup sour cream** |

Melt butter in a large skillet. Add onions and sauté until soft. Add cabbage and continue sautéing until the cabbage is crisp-tender. Add caraway seeds, salt and pepper. Cook noodles, drain and stir into cabbage. Add sour cream and cook for about 3 to 4 minutes longer.

 *These are my grandmother's recipes. She was Polish, born in Poland. They are a good example of the prevalence of pasta in seemingly widely different cultures.*

\*\*\*\*\*

## OYSTERS AND BRIE WITH PASTA

| | |
|---|---|
| **3 doz. small to medium oysters with their liquor** | **½ cup flour** |
| | **Salt, pepper and cayenne** |
| **2 cups cold water** | **1 lb. brie cheese** |
| **½ lb. unsalted butter** | **Pasta** |
| **1 cup finely chopped onions** | **1 cup heavy cream** |

Combine oysters and their liquor in cold water and refrigerate. Melt butter in a skillet over low heat. Add onions and sauté until they are soft. Add flour and whisk to make a white roux . Season with salt, pepper and cayenne.

In a saucepan, combine the oyster liquor and water together and bring to a boil. Temper the roux with the oyster / water liquid and then stir the roux into the liquid until well mixed. Turn heat to high, add cheese and stir until cheese begins to melt. Lower heat and cook 3 to 4 minutes or until mixture is smooth. Add cream and simmer to almost a boil for additional 2 minutes. Turn off heat. Add oysters and let stand for 3 to 4 minutes. Serve over your favorite pasta. Serves four.

 *This is a sturdy and fantastic meal! Make sure your don't curdle the cream. Keep the heat at a simmer. We like penne as our pasta for this, but you make want to use something different.*

\*\*\*\*\*

# SHRIMP AND MUSHROOMS WITH PASTA

**2 lb. fresh shrimp**
**¼ lb. butter**
**1 lb. fresh mushrooms, sliced**
**1 bunch scallions, chopped**
**1 clove garlic, finely minced**

**½ cup white wine**
**1 tbsp. fresh parsley, chopped**
**Salt**
**Freshly ground black pepper**

Clean, devein, wash and drain shrimp. Set aside

Melt butter in large skillet.  Add mushrooms, scallions, garlic and sauté until soft.

Add shrimp and continue cooking on medium to low heat until shrimp turn pink (3 to 4 minutes).  Add wine and parsley and cook an additional minute. Season with salt and pepper to taste.

Serve over your favorite pasta. Serves 4.

\*\*\*\*\*

# *BREAKFAST*

**EGGS BENEDICT** *ala Stella*
**FRATATA**
**HUEVOS RANCHERO**
**SPINACH OMELET**
**FRENCH TOAST**
**CHEESE TOAST**

# RISE AND SHINE

**I**'m an early morning riser. But this does not mean I'm totally awake when I rise. It takes awhile.

I normally get up between six and six thirty, shower, shave, and proceed to the kitchen. There, I fix coffee, orange juice, some toast, cream cheese and a little raspberry jam, a small dish of tapioca and then go sit on the porch or, if it's hot, the dining room and watch the sun come up.

I do all this in a sort of comatose state, moving from task to task by force of long years of habit. Jennie stays close behind me, following my meandering, sometimes staggering path even when it seems I'm obviously confused on exactly where I'm supposed to go.

As I move about, I hear the nails of her paws clicking faintly on the tiles of the kitchen floor. They make a pleasant sound in the soft morning quiet of the house. It penetrates my half awake state, giving me a sense of balance, reassuring the being or soul within me that there are wonderful things such as Jennie that are still there.

Sitting down for breakfast seems to ease my confusion. I then can just stare at the morning scene, the beach, the waters of the Sound, the gulls and to my east, the sun starting its rise.

Mind you, I'm not contemplating any world-shaking thoughts. Mostly, I'm just sitting, sipping my coffee, looking out on a world freshly touched by the slanting light of a new day's sun.

But I am doing something, something that is important to me, important in that otherwise I would have as easily stayed in bed for another hour or two.

I'm absorbing in a subliminal way the rising of the day, the feeling around me of new movement. I'm very gradually letting in a conscious feeling of all of this, of being alive and part of all the awakening that's happening all around me.

I don't think about this. I just let it slowly happen. Very slowly. And when it does, I'm ready.

I reach down and stroke Jennie sitting patiently beside me; I wave at a jogger going by on the beach road. I'm alive, I'm here, it's another day, and it feels good.

**... *PAUL***

## MY BREAKFAST RECIPES

*L*ike *many people, our normal weekday breakfast is solitary and light. I get up first, have a glass of buttermilk or orange juice and hurry off to work. As soon as I'm gone, Paul gets up and has his breakfast, which is usually tapioca, toast, orange juice and coffee.*

*It's on the weekends that we splurge on being with one another and have more expansive meals. Paul once described our weekend breakfasts as: "Eggs, or waffles with maple syrup, or both, thick bacon or spicy sausages, or both, home fries, grapefruit, orange juice, hot rolls with lots of butter and jam, coffee and Jennie under the table to keep our feet warm."*

*It sounds nice but with the pressure of weekend activities this usually only happens on one day of the weekend. This day is usually Sunday and the breakfast then is a leisurely one with newspapers and second cups of coffee (Paul) and tea (me).*

*These breakfasts are nice and we do look forward to when they take place. However, this chapter is not about those type of breakfasts.*

*This chapter is mostly about breakfasts for guests and special holidays such as Christmas. Some of the recipes that follow call for everyone to sit down en masse and eat as a festive group.*

*Others are for when you have guests that have scattered times as to when they get up. For these times, the recipes are for the key things to leave on a loaded sideboard for them to enjoy when they get up.*

*All of these are good breakfasts, some even grand. None of the ones I have included take long to prepare. This can be important when you have a house full of hungry guests or when unwrapping Christmas presents takes precedence.*

*So try them all and Bon Appetite.*

*... STELLA*

# EGGS BENEDICT *ala Stella*

### *Hollandaise Sauce*

| | |
|---|---|
| ¼ cup butter | ½ tsp. dry mustard |
| ¼ cup cream | ¼ tsp. salt |
| 2 egg yolks | Dash of Tabasco or 1/8 tsp. |
| 1 tbsp. freshly squeezed lemon | cayenne pepper |
| juice (fresh is essential) | |

Melt butter in glass bowl. Stir in rest of ingredients and microwave for 1 minute. Whip with wire whip every 15 seconds until light and fluffy

### *Egg Base*

| | |
|---|---|
| 8 large eggs | Hollandaise Sauce |
| 8 slices of French bread, slightly | 8 spears of asparagus, cooked |
| toasted and buttered | Orange slices |
| 8 slices of ham | |

Poach eggs. Place buttered, toasted bread on dish, two slices to a dish. Place a slice of ham on each bread slice. Drain eggs and place an egg atop each ham slice and top with Hollandaise sauce. Garnish each dish with asparagus and sliced oranges.

Serves 4.

.

*For a large group, expand recipe as needed and cook the poached eggs in advance. When you are about to prepare the other ingredients, place the previously cooked eggs in warm water to reheat them and proceed as above.*

*A variation of this would be to slice the ham in very thin slices. Lightly crisp each slice in a skillet and place several of these thin slices on each slice of bread. Add eggs and proceed as above.*

*****

# FRATATA

| | |
|---|---|
| 2 large potatoes | 8 large eggs |
| olive oil | 1 cup milk |
| ½ cup chopped scallions | 1 cup shredded cheddar cheese |
| 1 large tomato sliced | Salt and pepper |

Bake potatoes in microwave and slice into ¼" slices. Spray a large skillet or casserole dish with olive oil. Line skillet or dish with potatoes. Sprinkle scallions over potatoes and add tomatoes in an even layer. Put aside.

Place eggs in a large bowl and whisk until a pale yellow color. Add milk and blend thoroughly. Add shredded cheese. Season with salt and pepper. Mix until all ingredients are blended. Pour mixture over potatoes and scallions.

If recipe is in a casserole dish, place in 350 degree oven until done. If in a skillet, cook on stove top on low to medium heat until set (move ingredients around ever so slightly to get mixture to cook thoroughly without disturbing its overall appearance).

Remove from oven or skillet and serve. Serves 4 to 6.

*This is a dish we learned to like when we traveled in Spain. It was usually cut into serving sized pieces and placed between two thick slices of freshly baked bread and served as a sandwich. If you like, you can add bacon or ham to the dish and serve in wedges. It makes a good sturdy meal and goes nicely with toast and coffee or tea,.*

*This can be served hot or at room temperature and is a great dish to place out on the sideboard for your guests breakfast. Put out with crisped ham and / or bacon, an assortment of fruit and toast.*

*\*\*\*\*\**

## *HUEVOS RANCHERO*

| | |
|---|---|
| **Flour tortillas** | **4 large eggs** |
| **4 to 6 pieces thinly sliced ham** | **4 slice ham, thinly sliced** |
| **1 cup boiled rice** | **1 cup salsa** |
| **1 cup pinto beans, cooked** | **¾ cup shredded cheese** |

Sauté tortillas, drain and set aside. Fry ham until crispy. Place 2 tortillas flat on an ovenproof dish. Place three mounds consisting of rice, ham, and beans across the tortillas in a line (with ham in center). Fry eggs (two per serving) sunny side up and place on top of the rice, ham, and beans. Spoon salsa over eggs and top with cheese..

Place under the broiler until the cheese has melted and the eggs have cooked every so slightly. Serve immediately with additional tortillas (heated) and butter.

Serves two.

*This is particularly good when served with a rather sweetish, hot salsa. It also makes a very good late breakfast or brunch. This kind of meal is very filling and should keep everyone from wanting something until much later in the day.*

*****

# SPINACH OMELET

| | |
|---|---|
| **8 large leaves of spinach** | **4 large eggs** |
| **4 scallions, finely sliced** | **½ cup milk** |
| **4 large mushrooms, sliced thin** | **2 tbsp. butter.** |
| **Salt, pepper and garlic powder** | **½ cup cheddar cheese, shredded.** |

Julienne spinach leaves and add scallions and mushrooms. Season with salt, pepper and garlic powder. Set aside.

Place eggs in a glass bowl and whisk until light and fluffy. Add milk and continue whisking.

Heat skillet until hot and add one tablespoon butter and melt. Immediately add half of egg mixture and swirl around pan until mixture begins to cook and set. Place a row of the vegetable mixture in a line across the pan and top with cheese. Fold the eggs up from both sides and let cook until they can be flipped.

Cook every so slightly on other side and turn onto a serving dish.

Serve immediately. Serves two.

*This makes a very substantial breakfast, but to be truthful, I often make it as a fast supper when I find myself running and time becoming a little thin. Paul doesn't complain and gladly eats it for either meal. Serve with some home fries on the side and you are set for either breakfast or supper!*

**\*\*\*\*\***

## FRENCH TOAST

| | |
|---|---|
| **2 small eggs** | **Olive oil** |
| **3/4 cup milk** | **½ loaf day-old French bread,** |
| **1 tsp. Vanilla extract** | **sliced 1/2 to 3/4" thick** |
| **2 tbsp. of butter** | |

Place eggs, milk and vanilla in a bowl and whisk until frothy. Set aside.

Heat a skillet on medium heat and melt butter. Increase heat and add about a tablespoon of oil so that the butter doesn't burn. Dip slices of French bread into egg/milk mixture just long enough to coat both sides.

Place coated bread in skillet to cook until both sides are nicely browned. Drain on paper towels and keep warm in an oven until you have cooked all that you need. Normally, four slices of bread is more than adequate per serving.

Serve this with the typical breakfast sides of bacon, ham or sausage. Serves two.

 *Make sure you use day-old bread. Fresh bread will sop up the egg mixture and give you soft, mushy toast. French bread is best in my estimation, but regular white loaf bread that is a day or so old does almost as well.*

 *You can serve the toast with fresh blueberries, strawberries, raspberries or peaches that have been macerated. However, we prefer to stick with the traditional butter and maple syrup. I manage to have some good Pennsylvania maple syrup on hand at all times. The syrup usually comes to me through the good graces of my Pennsylvania family and friends or as a result of one of my "shopping trips" back home when I look for the things I just can't get in Mississippi. But, such trips work two ways – lots of good Mississippi things go back with me to Pennsylvania.*

**\*\*\*\*\***

## *CHEESE TOAST*

½ loaf French or Italian bread     1 cup shredded cheddar cheese
2 tbsp. soft butter                Romano or Parmesan Cheese
6 slices fried bacon or ham

Slice bread the long way and remove some of the bulk. Butter bread
and toast it in oven just long enough for butter to melt. Remove bread
from oven and top with the bacon or ham. Sprinkle cheese liberally on
top of bacon/ham and return to oven to melt and brown the cheese.

Serve immediately. Serves two.

 *If you want to add a little more zest to the toast with very little
effort, thinly slice some Parmesan or Romano cheese and put
the slices on top of the cheddar just before you return it to the
oven.*

 *This makes a simple and fulfilling breakfast along with some
fresh fruit and your favorite beverage. Great for a busy
Saturday when you want to sit together for a simple breakfast
that doesn't require a lot of preparation.*

\*\*\*\*\*

*Stella and Paul La Violette*

# SANDWICHES

*AVOCADO AND BACON SANDWICH*
*A GOOD SALAMI SANDWICH*
*PAUL'S FAVORITE TOMATO SANDWICH*
*PAN-FRIED GRILLED CHEESE*
*ROAST BEEF PO'BOY*
*OYSTER PO'BOY*

# LAISSEZ LES BON TEMPS ROULER

**S**tella and I were on the front porch roof working on the sun-warped redwood siding of the house, pulling out nails and putting in screws. A head popped up the ladder and watched us. It was Don, our neighbor. "Is this a private party or can anyone play?"

"You can play." I said, "Grab a pry bar." With his help the job went quickly, and soon Stella went down to make lunch. Just as we finished the last plank, Stella came back up with lemonade and avocado and bacon sandwiches.

We sat there, letting the March sun warm us, looking out over the water, drinking the lemonade and eating the sandwiches. "We have company," said Stella. On the beach road, a car with Wisconsin tags had stopped. Two men — one with a camcorder — got out.

"Hi!" yelled the driver, waving. "What are you people doing up there?"

Don stood up and toasted the men with his lemonade, "We're partying, man."

"On the roof?"

"We're having a roof party," Don said. "Don't you people party in Wisconsin?"

The man laughed, "Not on our roofs."

"No kidding? Man, you guys are missing something up there. Here, we do it all the time. *Laissez les bon temps rouler* - Let the good times roll."

"Can we take your picture?" said the man with the camcorder. "This may be normal to you, but they won't believe it back home."

We yelled sure and they took our picture as we saluted them with our lemonade. They laughed, waved goodbye and left.

It didn't take long before roof parties were common around the neighborhood. It was a cool spring and it was fun to sit up high, with friends, something cool to drink, and "sing songs and tell lies".

Then came my downfall. We were on Lee's mildly sloped roof. All ages and sizes. Even little Shannon, Henry's 7 year old daughter was up there, tooting an annoying long, plastic horn.

I had had my two-beer limit when Shannon came by loudly tooting. "Shannon, let me show you something,"

"I don't trust you, Uncle Paul," she said.

"No, no, I want to show you a trick," I said remembering a fraternity drinking trick shown to me by a Navy pilot. "Let me have the horn and get Don to bring over a beer." Don came and I popped the beer can lid, put the can on one end of the horn and raising the horn to my mouth, I tilted my head back, elevating the horn straight up in the air.

Glug! Swoosh! The can of beer was empty.

"God!" said Don. "Lee, come here and see this. Bring a beer." Lee came over and I repeated the chug-a-lug. Henry came up and wanted also to see me do it. Don handed me another beer. I looked at it and suddenly, began not to feel too well. "I'll do it in a bit, but I have to go back to the house, I forgot something," and I began climbing down from the roof.

"Where is he going?" asked Henry. "I want to see the trick." "Uncle Paul has to go to potty," said Shannon.

I hurried to the house and into the living room. Gretal was sleeping on the floor. She woke when I came in and looked up, her tail wagging.

I decided she had the right idea and lay down beside her. However, once I positioned myself, Gretal with an audible "hmpff," got up and walked away.

In a little while, I heard Stella in the kitchen, she was back from shopping and she was talking to Gretal. "Where's Daddy?" She followed Gretal into the living room,

"Oh, there you are. I thought you'd be up on the roof at Lee's. They're having a party."

I said, "Mmm."

"Oh, I see. You've already been up there."

I said, "Mmm."

"This is it." She went and got a blanket ... "You could have killed yourself" ... and threw it over me ... "The whole roof thing is stupid." ... and put a small pillow under my head. "No more roof parties. Understand? No more roof parties."

She went back in the kitchen. Gretal followed her.

So, that was the end of the roof parties. It was getting warm anyway.

But sometimes, when I'm up on the roof, sweeping leaves from the gutters, or putting up the shade cloths, I sit down and pull a coke out of my nail apron and relax, feeling the warm roof under me, watch a squirrel steal one of my pecans, a mockingbird chase another mockingbird and see the sun hitting the water so that every so often I catch a flashing flicker of light.

Then I pull the tab on the can, toast the wind, the birds, the water and have a roof party just by myself.

## *... PAUL*

# MY SANDWICH RECIPES

*M*aking *a good sandwich is an easygoing, fun type of adventure. By appearing to be a quick meal, something to be almost slapped together and eaten quickly, sandwiches are not usually taken seriously.*

*There are good reasons for this. When Paul goes into the house and takes salami out of the refrigerator, jams some slices between two pieces of bread and walks back out, we are talking about the extremes of quick and simple. In fact, by the time he has returned to whatever he was doing, his salami sandwich is usually gone.*

*I'm not talking about those kinds of sandwiches in this chapter. While my sandwiches here still follow the theme of simplicity as the rest of my recipes, they do take a little more time and thought. But the ones I have included are fun and should be considered for what they are meant to be; the main part of a relaxed meal. So be my guest; try them in that spirit.*

*A couple of things: I like to spray my olive oil on those sandwiches that require oil. I use a pretty blue little spray bottle I picked up for less than two dollars at K Mart. Also fresh, crisp, tasty bread is an absolute everything to many of my sandwich recipes. Take time to make sure you get a fresh, crisp loaf or roll. Shop around till you find a store that can provide this quality of bread to you. Believe it or not, these store do exist. Bread freezes well. So, stock up on bread and put it in the freezer and defrost it when it is needed.*

*Believe it or not, how you cut your sandwich is important. I like to cut my plain bread sandwiches diagonally. This cuts through everything and gives a more uniform look to the sandwich presentation. Cut your po'boys into easily handled sizes but not too small. I usually cut them at right angles but most people cut them at an angle. Whatever.*

*Please, never, never heat up or cook a sandwich in a microwave. No sandwich, no matter how quickly it is wanted, should be mistreated that way.*

*... STELLA*

## AVOCADO AND BACON SANDWICH

| | |
|---|---|
| 2 tbsp. mayonnaise | Salt and pepper to taste |
| 4 slices white bread, slightly toasted | Squeeze of lemon juice |
| 1 large ripe avocado (not overly ripe) | 8 strips of crisply fried bacon |

Spread mayonnaise on each slice of bread. Peel and slice avocado in long slices about ¼" thick and place on one slice of bread. Season with salt and pepper and a small squeeze of lemon juice. Place four slices of bacon on top of avocados and then add the top slice of bread to complete the sandwich.

Slice and serve. Serves two.

 *This goes good best with regular loaf white bread. Lightly toast the bread for crispness.*

 *This sandwich is extremely good and amazingly enough is just the result of having "nothing in the refrigerator to eat on an early Saturday morning."*

*****

# A GOOD SALAMI SANDWICH

1 loaf of crusty French bread , fresh
2 tbsp. mayonnaise
½ lb. Genoa salami, sliced extra thin
1 tomato, sliced
1 med.  sweet onion, thinly  sliced
Olive oil

Balsamic vinegar
Salt
Freshly ground black
  pepper
3 leaves Romaine lettuce
  (optional)

Lightly toast bread.   Spread the bread with mayonnaise.  Layer salami slices (be generous), tomato and sweet onion on bread  and lightly spray with olive oil.  Add a dash or two of balsamic vinegar and season with salt and freshly ground black pepper.

Dress with Romaine lettuce leaves if desired. Serves 3 to 4.

 *The secret here, as it is in all good sandwiches, is the bread. It has to be both fresh and crisp. This is extremely important. Don't compromise on the quality of the bread you include in your sandwich if you really intend to make a good sandwich. Search around. Find a good bakery and use their bread in your "good" sandwiches. What is fantastic is to use warm bread just out of the baker's oven.*

 *To be extra good, the salami must be sliced extremely thin. I don't know why it is so, but cutting it extra thin for a sandwich makes a world of difference. Try it.*

\*\*\*\*\*

# PAUL'S FAVORITE TOMATO SANDWICH

| | |
|---|---|
| **1 large garden fresh tomato** | **Salt** |
| **Mayonnaise** | **Coarsely ground black pepper** |
| **2 slices regular loaf white bread** | |

Slice tomato in ¼" slices. Spread mayonnaise on two slices of regular loaf bread and place slices of tomato on one slice. Season with salt and ground pepper. Top with the other slice of bread and cut sandwich in two.

Makes one serving.

 *This is a wonderful way to use those just-reached-their peak-of-ripeness-tomatoes from your garden or the farmers' market. When the tomatoes start to get ripe, this sandwich to Paul is like catnip to our black tom, Holly*

 *For those of you who may not be mayonnaise fans, you can substitute butter and achieve an equally good effect. Also, note that coarse ground black pepper rather than finely ground black pepper provides a stronger flavor that substantially adds to the sandwich.*

*Many bad things have been said about American regular loaf white bread. In many cases it is true that crispy French or Italian bread is better tasting than regular loaf bread. However, this is Paul's sandwich and he insists that the tenderness inherent in regular loaf white bread is essential to this sandwich, that the bread allows the rich flavor of the ripe tomato to come into its own resulting in a rich superior tasting sandwich.*

*I've tried his sandwich and I've found, that strange as it seems, what he says is true.*

\*\*\*\*\*

## PAN-FRIED GRILLED CHEESE

**4 slices cheddar cheese**　　　　　**Oil**
**4 slices regular loaf white bread**　**1 tomato, sliced**
**Butter**　　　　　　　　　　　　**Salt and pepper**

Place cheese on bread and make two sandwiches. Butter each side of sandwiches with soft butter.  Heat a skillet on medium heat and melt some butter and gradually add some olive oil so that it covers the bottom of the skillet very lightly.

Add sandwiches to skillet and brown both sides slowly until bread is crispy.  Remove from skillet and open each sandwich. Place a thick slice of tomato inside of each and season with salt and pepper. Quickly close sandwiches  and cut in half or quarters.

Serve immediately. Serves two.

 *This is a very tasty, easy to prepare sandwich and is particularly good when you can go out in the garden and get a nice fresh ripe tomato to enhance its flavor.  Use fresh ground pepper for the seasoning and see just how good it can be.*

*For variation with the tomato insert, try using crisp bacon or similarly crisp ham left over from breakfast.*

*****

### ROAST BEEF PO'BOY

¼ lb. of butter
2 med. onions, sliced
1 loaf po'boy bread

Brown gravy (see frog hint)
½ lb. thinly sliced roast beef
Tabasco

Melt about 3 tablespoons butter in a heavy skillet. Add sliced onions and sauté until brown. Cut po'boy bread in half the long way and spread with remaining butter. Lightly toast bread in oven. Spread small amount of gravy on bread. Add a layer of very thinly sliced roast beef and more brown gravy. Sprinkle lightly with Tabasco sauce. Top roast beef with onions. Pour more gravy over onions and top with other side of bread.

Cut into serving size pieces and serve with plenty of paper napkins.

Makes four generous servings.

 *I usually use a rump roast for the base of this sandwich and it is also a good way to use up the remains of a Sunday roast. The secret here is to slice the roast very thin and then stack it on heavy. The brown gravy is made from the roast's pan drippings.*

*I try to keep a quantity of the gravy for several other uses in addition to the po'boy. For instance, brown gravy is delicious served over the French fries that normally would accompany the po'boy. Serve with some good kosher dill pickles.*

\*\*\*\*\*

# OYSTER PO'BOY

**1 quart shucked oysters, drained and dried**
**3 eggs**
**4 tbspn. water**
**Seasoned bread crumbs**

**1 loaf po'boy bread**
**Butter**
**Salt, pepper and cayenne**
**Tabasco sauce**

Dry oysters between some paper towels. Beat eggs and water together. Dip oysters in the egg mix and then in breadcrumbs and again in egg mix and again in breadcrumbs. Let oysters dry on a rack for about 30 minutes. Fry them in oil at 375 degrees. Remove from oil and drain on paper towels.

Slice po'boy loaf in half and butter generously with butter. Toast in oven until lightly browned. Spread oysters over bread and season to taste with salt and pepper.

Sprinkle lightly with Tabasco sauce and serve. Makes 4 generous servings.

  *Consider this as a generic seafood po'boy recipe. Fresh fish or shrimp, cooked in the same manner as the oysters, will give you a fish or shrimp po'boy. A good 'half and half' is to have a shrimp and oyster po'boy.*

 *These po'boys can also be dressed with shredded lettuce and sliced tomato. Mayonnaise can be substituted for the butter. Also, save the oyster liquor - it can be used in other soups or stews.*

\*\*\*\*\*

## STEAK BURGERS

**1 lb. sirloin steak**                    **Worcestershire sauce**
**Salt and pepper**

Chill steak and put through a meat grinder for a medium grind. Season with salt, pepper and Worcestershire sauce. Form into thick patties and place in a slightly oiled skillet. Cook on high heat initially in order to seer the burger on both side, thereby sealing in all the good juices. Cook the burgers at a lower temperature to the desired degree of "doneness" (please, out of respect for the thoughts that have gone into this book, *never* overcook).

Place on slightly toasted Kaiser rolls (with seeds if available) and dress to taste with fresh tomato, onions, lettuce, a little mayonnaise, relish.

Makes 4 generous servings.

*As you turn the burger for the last time, place a slice of Gorgonzola cheese on top and let it melt while the burger finishes cooking. Adds a delightful little zip to the burger.*

*Ever wonder why the fast hamburger places have to put bacon, barbeque sauce and other strong flavored ingredients atop their hamburgers? Sanitary codes dictate that all hamburgers must be thoroughly cooked( i.e., well past well done) to avoid the possibility of salmonella. Since hamburgers cooked this way taste very much like packing case plastic filler, the fast food venders are forced to add the strong flavored additions.*

*Since we like our burgers cooked medium rare (Paul) and medium (me), I grind the meat for the burgers we cook at home. By being extra careful, there is little chance of their being contaminated with salmonella (clean your grinder thoroughly after each use and always rinse before using).*

*****

# *DRINKS*

### *ORANGE FRAPPES*
### *FRUIT JUICE & TONIC SPRITZ*
### *SUN TEA*
### *SANGRIA*
### *HOT RUM TODDY*
### *MULLED WINE*
### *MEXICAN HOT CHOCOLATE*
### *EGGNOG ala Stella*

# *OAKS, LOUNGES AND SUMMER DRINKS AND ICES*

In early spring, we invariably get hit by strong southerly gales and the salt-laden spray "burns" the new leaves of the large live oaks around our house. Luckily, new leaves are quick to replace those that are badly burnt.

Live oaks are an ambient fixture to life here. These beautiful, stately trees are found all along the beaches of the Mississippi Coast, providing a green contrast to the white sandy beaches.

These are very hardy trees that grow some 50 feet in height and have broad canopies that often cover 100 feet. These large long-living oaks with their dangling silver gray growths of "Spanish moss" – actually an air plant of the same bromeliad family as the pineapple – have a peculiar place in the hearts of the people of the Coast.

Stella and I are lucky to have a number of live oaks growing about the house; two of these are old enough to be registered by the Hancock County Historical Society. The Historical Society's requirement is that in order to be registered a tree must be more than 100 years old as determined by their circumference five feet above the ground. These measurements indicate that our trees are 165 and 235 years old.

A pleasant extra that came with registering the trees is that you can give them names. We've named them after Weimaraners that in times past have been very dear to us. On each tree trunk is a small green registry sign with the name "Miss Gretal" on one and "Miss Heidi" on the other. If we had been here in 1814, we could have sat in the branches of a fifty-year-old "Miss Heidi" and watched the British row by in their boats to attempt and fail in their assault of New Orleans.

**114**

Stella and I have discovered a natural breezeway beside the porch at the east corner of the house. We've taken advantage of this by laying down a low wooden deck beside the porch and between two live oaks, one of which is "Miss Gretal".

A peculiarity of live oaks is their tendency to send out low branches just above the ground. These can be as much as three feet in diameter and extend thirty or more feet from the trunk.

There is one such low branch growing off of Miss Gretal that snakes about two feet above the wooden deck, splitting its available space in two. Because of its oddity, we have decided to leave it there.

As such branches go, it is still small, being only about six to eight inches in diameter. With some heavy wire, Stella and I have been training it to make a right turn at the sidewalk to the gazebo, so that it runs parallel to the walk. It appears to be accommodating us and is growing in that direction.

We and the tree have been at this now for about ten years. We feel that in another twenty or so years we will have a nice natural bench to sit on when we walk to the gazebo. It's something to look forward to. Till then, one of our grandchildren, Lorelei, and our black tomcat, Holly, use the branch to gain access to the upper limbs of the tree. So the branch is being used while we wait.

Stella has slung a hammock between the two oaks and I have positioned a chaise lounge and a small table on the deck. We use the table for drinks and dishes of Stella's ice creams and summer ices or sorbets. The set up on a whole is very comfortable.

Over the years, we have spent many of our early evenings here, relaxing, talking, and doing other necessary things. When asked, we tell people that we're "training the tree".

*...PAUL*

*Stella and Paul La Violette*

# MY DRINK RECIPES

*I know it is easy to use canned beverages at a meal or just to have a tall glass of iced water. Then there are alcoholic beverages in boxes, bottles and cans of wines and beers. All of these are beyond the realm of this book as being too simple or more involved (some of the wines) than I care to go into.*

*However, there are several drinks that go with lunches or special occasions that Paul and I drink that may be of interest. I have included them in this chapter for completeness to the overall structure of this book.*

*Don't be put off by the seeming insipidness of some of these such as Sun Tea and Juice Spritzes. These are very refreshing drinks that offer a very good alternative to the canned colas those ads everywhere seem to demand we drink.*

*Some of the drinks are nice on a cold winter day. While our winters are usually mild, there are occasional cold days when a hot toddy or mulled wine is just the thing to have.*

*Cheers!*

## ... STELLA

## ORANGE FRAPPES

| | |
|---|---|
| 2 large egg (optional) | 6 tbsp. heavy cream |
| 12 oz. orange juice | 1 tsp. vanilla extract |
| 4 tbsp. powdered sugar | 2 cup crushed ice |

Place eggs in blender and whip. Add orange juice, powdered sugar, cream and vanilla. Whip all ingredients until thoroughly mixed. Add crushed ice and mix again until mixture is fairly smooth. DO NOT OVER MIX. Taste. You may prefer more sugar depending on the acidity of the orange juice.

Serve immediately. Serves two.

 *This is a great refreshing drink on a hot summer day and, since it is filling, it is often a substitute for lunch at our house or when we are cruising on the porch. Also a great energy booster. While the egg is strictly optional, we like it and always include it. It does give a nice creamy, thick consistency to the drink.*

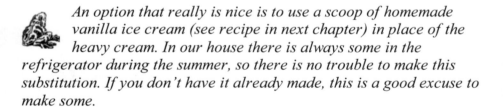 *An option that really is nice is to use a scoop of homemade vanilla ice cream (see recipe in next chapter) in place of the heavy cream. In our house there is always some in the refrigerator during the summer, so there is no trouble to make this substitution. If you don't have it already made, this is a good excuse to make some.*

 *Other fruit juices can be used, but we like orange the best. Experiment after you get the hang of making this recipe and see which you prefer.*

*****

## FRUIT JUICE & TONIC SPRITZ

**6 ice cubes**
**12 oz. orange (or grapefruit, or grape, or apple, or**
**cranberry, or ….) juice (preferably not from concentrate)**
**6 oz. tonic water**

Place ice cubes in large glasses or tumblers.  Add orange juice and stir.
Add tonic water and stir  again until thoroughly mixed.

Serve immediately. Serves two.

 *This is a quick but good and refreshing summer drink.  It is
more effective in thirst quenching than any of the canned
carbonated beverages and is a real energy booster.*

*Feel free to try almost any other fruit juices. Explore. Paul tells me that
apple juice is particularly good, but I haven't tried it.*

**\*\*\*\*\***

# SUN TEA

**1 gallon water**
**6 tea bags**

Place cold water in a transparent gallon container (glass or plastic) container and add tea bags.  Place container in a sunny location and let tea steep for about four or five hours.  Bring container back in the house, remove tea bags and refrigerate.

*This sounds like a rather simplistic recipe for a cookbook, but it is a very important one for those of us who live down here on the Gulf Coast.  It doesn't require you to boil the tea, thus eliminating unneeded humidity and heat from your kitchen.*

*Making tea this way results in a superior ice tea than that produced by boiling. This method makes tea with a wonderful, non-bitter flavor, which keeps under refrigeration for almost forever.  We keep a gallon of sun tea in the refrigerator all summer long (not the same batch of course).*

*You can sweeten it or serve with a little lemon wedge and some fresh mint for a very refreshing summer drink.*

*****

## SANGRIA

| | |
|---|---|
| 1/4 cup sugar | Fresh fruit of your choice (oranges, |
| 1/4 cup brandy | lemons, apples, limes, peaches, etc.). |
| 1 fresh orange, juiced | 1 liter wine (red, white or rose). |
| 1 fresh lemon, juiced | 12 oz. Seltzer water |

In a small container combine sugar, brandy, orange and lemon juice: Shake or stir until sugar is dissolved. Slice assorted fruit and place in large pitcher. Pour sugar brandy juice mix over the fresh fruit. Add wine. Place in refrigerator for 1 hour.

Add seltzer just before serving. Serve in tall glasses containing several ice cubes and some of the fruit. Serves 8.

*\*\*\*\*\**

## HOT RUM TODDY

| | |
|---|---|
| 4 cups water | 1 tspn freshly grated nutmeg |
| ½ cup dark brown sugar | 1 fresh lemon, juiced |
| ¼ lb. butter | 2 cups dark rum |
| 1 clove | 4 cinnamon sticks |

Bring water to near boil. Add and stir in sugar, butter, clove, nutmeg and lemon juice.

Remove from heat. Add rum. Pour into fancy mugs, add cinnamon sticks and serve. Serves 4.

 *If you have a fire going in the fireplace and your guests are around the fire, have a clean poker sitting in the flames. When someone's drink has become cold, pull the poker out and with, the proper flourish, stick it in his or her drink!. Remember you will get only one flourish to a drink, then you will have to reheat poker.*

*\*\*\*\*\**

## MULLED WINE

| | |
|---|---|
| **Sugar** | **1/2 gal. water** |
| **20 whole cloves** | **2 tsp. grated orange peel** |
| **Half a cinnamon stick** | **1 tsp. grated lemon peel** |
| **3 crushed nutmeg** | **1 gal. red wine** |

Add sugar, cloves, cinnamon, and nutmeg to water. Boil for 5 minutes. Strain the syrup into a large pot, and add the citrus peelings. Mix and bring to a boil. Add more sugar if needed. Add wine. Cook for another 10 minutes on a small flame, filter out the spices and serve hot.

Serves many.

*This is a good drink to have ready for your guests on a cold day during the holidays. An extra touch would be to add a cup of rum and / or brandy or both.*

*As with the hot toddy, if you have a fire going in the fireplace and your guests are around the fire, have a clean poker sitting in the flames. When someone's wine has become cold, pull the poker out and, with the proper flourish, stick it in his or her drink!*

**\*\*\*\*\***

## MEXICAN HOT CHOCOLATE

**1 oz. unsweetened chocolate**          **½ tsp. of cinnamon**
**1 tbsp. sugar**                                    **2 cups of milk**
**Pinch of salt**

Combine all the ingredients and cook over hot water until chocolate melts. Beat until foamy and pour into cups.

Serves two.

*You can also make this in the traditional Mexican manner by using a Mexican beater called a molinillo. Follow the recipe up to the point of the beating process. Pour the mixture into a pitcher and place the molinillo in the pitcher. Grasp the handle of the molinillo between the palms of your hands and twirl it until the mixture becomes foamy. Pour in cups or mugs and serve.*

*On a cool winter evening, it's a fun and an entertaining utensil to bring out when you have friend over for some dessert and hot chocolate. Buenas tardes! y Ole!*

*****

## *EGGNOG ala Stella*

12 eggs, separated                1 fifth brandy
1 qt. half and half               12 oz. bourbon or whiskey
1 pt. heavy cream                 2 ½ cups granulated sugar
1 pt. light cream                 Nutmeg
½ gal. milk (whole)               Homemade vanilla ice
1 fifth rum                       cream (optional)

Separate eggs and beat whites until stiff.  Beat yolks.  Fold whites into yolks.  Add half and half, creams and milk to egg mixture and stir well (do not beat).  Add rum, brandy, bourbon/whiskey and sugar and stir well.  Ladle into glass jars for storage.  Keeps a week to 10 days in the refrigerator.

Shake well before serving.  Just before serving add small scoop of ice cream (optional) and sprinkle fresh grated nutmeg on the top.

Makes 7 ½ to 8 quarts.

*This is a large recipe for a holiday party, but you can make a batch of the base mix and keep it in the refrigerator for when one or two friends drop by during the holidays. For this use, just add the other ingredients when you are ready to serve. You will have to beat some fresh egg whites, but that should be just a little additional effort for an excellent drink. Also, while serving this at a party, try to keep the punch bowl surrounded by some ice. The coolness enhances the flavor and retains the fluffiness of the drink.*

*The ice cream option is nice when there are only a few guests rather than when there is a large gathering. . In our house there is always some in the refrigerator, so there is no trouble to include. If you don't have it already made, this is a good excuse to make some. It comes in handy during the holidays.*

\*\*\*\*\*

# *DESSERTS*

*POUND CAKE*
*COUNTRY STYLE VANILLA*
*  ICE CREAM*
*WHIPPED CREAM TOPPING*
*STELLA'S LEMON ICE*
*CHEESECAKE*
*FROZEN PEACH(OR ANY*
*  FRUIT) DESSERT*

*CHOCOLATE MOUSSE*
*MAYONNAISE ICE CREAM*
*PAUL'S TURNOVERS*
*PIZZELLES*
*PINEAPPLE WALNUT CAKE*
*PINEAPPLE CREAM PIE*
*CARMEL FLAN*
*KRUSCIKI*

# BLUEBERRY PEACHES,
# STRAWBERRY JAM

**W**hen I was a young boy in the Navy stationed in Newport, Rhode Island, I went for a while with a girl from Fall River, Massachusetts. She wasn't a very pretty girl, but she was pleasant, fun to be with, and when she let me kiss her, her kisses were a pure and wondrous delight.

To me Mississippi peaches are a lot like that. If you put Mississippi peaches up beside the peaches produced by our neighboring states, they don't look as good. They're small, they don't travel easily, there isn't as much fruit to each peach; but once you take a bite ... Wow! They have a wonderful pure peach flavor, they're sweet, they drip with juice ...

I love the time in the spring of the year when they come into season and you can buy them from the road vendors. That's the problem. There is no use going to the Save-a-Center. These chain stores won't carry them because of their puny looks.

You have to look for them being sold by the side of the road and the vendors selling real Mississippi peaches are hard to find. Many try to sell you bad - looking Georgia or Alabama peaches and to be honest, a bad Georgia or Alabama peach is a bad peach.

There is a place near Woolmarket where Stella takes me to on occasion to pick blueberries. Now, I like blueberries with my waffles and in muffins. They're good toppings for a lots of things or alone with just sugar and heavy cream, they're delicious. So I say ok, to please Stella, and I go with her.

I'm really not too good at picking any kind of fruit and blueberries are no exception. Mostly I sample and look for bushes that have a lot of berries and find after a bit that my bucket is only half full and Stella has already picked two buckets. But it's nice out in the quiet of the country and I don't complain.

It's what happens afterward that I like.

Beside the large shed where the farmer weighs your buckets is a small tree loaded with Mississippi peaches. The farmer doesn't like to sell the peaches; "There aren't enough for me to sell and for me and my wife to have some, too" But he usually gives me a basket free and I go home loaded with fresh blueberries and a little bit of heaven.

Stella is good at making preserves and jams out of these seasonal fruits. Blueberries are good, but she goes hog wild with strawberries and these have to be "fresh", meaning we pick them. Now picking strawberries is not like picking blueberries. The berries don't seem to be as accessible and Stella can tell when I'm looking at a hawk or eating too many of my pickings.

But it gets done and that night she whips up some cream, treats the strawberries with sugar in a way to generate a little syrup with the berries and we have coffee and dessert out on the porch and watch the day end. What strawberries that are left over, she preserves. Therein lies a bit of family lore.

One year Stella made a batch of strawberries that gave us about a dozen pint-sized jars of preserves. When she looked at them the next day, she was disgusted. She had evidently made some small error in her usual recipe. The preserves appeared runny and, while they had good color, they didn't seem right to her.

She was going to throw the whole batch out when I happened by and tasted them. !!!!! Unbelievable! I'm not a strawberry person; but the preserves she had made from those particular strawberries were good!

For much of that summer, I put the preserves on about anything that laid flat on the table. Stella's pound cake and whipped cream were heavily involved in this and it was a wonderful summer. But, sooner than I thought could be possible, the jars of those fantastic strawberry preserves were all gone.

"I thought you made a dozen jars?" I asked. "I did, but I gave some away," she said. "Now what's wrong? Where are you going?"

"I'm going out back to check! Maybe you gave away my pickup, too!"

"Don't be silly. I can make some more.. Quite sulking."

But she couldn't. And, as much as she tried in the years since, she hasn't been able to.

Thomas Wolfe said that you can't go home. Maybe he was referring to a greater mystery than a house in some distant town, maybe he was referring to my never being able to have any more of that wonderful batch of strawberry preserve, or maybe kisses from that long ago girl from Fall River.

But I do know this.

Out toward Woolmarket there is a blueberry farm. And beside the large shed where they weigh your buckets, there is a peach tree. And if you go there at the right time of year and sit and talk a bit with the farmer, he'll let you have some of his peaches.

*...PAUL*

# MY DESSERT RECIPES

*I* think that this, of all the chapters in this book, is the chapter that I enjoyed writing the most. The dishes here are, as with the others, easy to fix. But beyond that, they are all wonderfully delicious.

Paul agrees with me on this. He has tried them all out at one time or another (sometimes, for example the pound cake and ice cream recipes, many, many, many times) and has suggested that I preface the chapter with the following advice :

> **Warning! All of the following recipes are delicious. Some are so delicious as to be addictive and must be eaten with a reasonable degree of caution. Please don't serve this to your husband, children or close friends without giving them these same words of caution.**

But now that I have said that, don't let it put you off. Go ahead and pick and choose among these recipes and indulge yourself. Life on all too rare occasions has some exceptional high points and when we find ourselves present among these high points we should stay and enjoy them. I think that some of these deserts can easily make you reach those high points.

So, be my guest, stay and enjoy, and, as I've said before,

*Bon Appetit.*

*... STELLA*

## POUND CAKE

| | |
|---|---|
| **1 lb. butter** | **3 ½ cups cake flour** |
| **2 2/3 cups sugar** | **½ cup whipping cream** |
| **8 eggs, separated** | **1 tsp. vanilla** |

Bring all ingredients to room temperature (this is important as it promotes the fluffiness of the cake). Lightly grease a very large tube pan and set aside. Reserve 1/3 cup sugar for egg whites. Separate the eggs.

Cream butter thoroughly, adding sugar gradually. Continue to beat for 10 minutes. Add egg yolks, one at a time, beating well after each addition..

Sift flour 3 times and then add alternately with the whipping cream and vanilla. Beat for another 10 minutes until mixture is very light. Beat egg whites separately until frothy and gradually add in 1/3 cup sugar. Fold egg whites into the batter.

Pour batter into tube pan and bake at 300° F for 1 and ¾ hours or until it is done (crust should spring back to touch). Let cool in pan for 10 minutes and then turn out and cool on rack. Do not try to remove before cake has had a chance to properly cool.

 *Please, for best results, do not substitute any of the ingredients in this recipe.*

 *I usually serve the cake plain and in very thin slices. I find that thin slices are a definite plus to bringing out the cakes flavor make the cake seem lighter and fluffier.*

*This is a wonderful cake. Its flavor is delicate, however it is easily overpowered by the wrong accompaniment. It is **NOT** as good served with ice cream as ice cream tends to overpower the delicate flavor of the cake. It can be given a lemon glaze if desired, but we usually don't do this for the same reason.*

*However, the cake **is GOOD** served with fresh sweetened strawberries and whipped cream. These seem to compliment rather than detract from the cake. Paul's favorite to add with these is Grand Marnier.*

*The beauty about this cake is that it can be frozen for months, then defrosted as good as new! Since it is difficult for Paul and I to finish a whole cake in the three or so days it takes to dry out, I usually freeze it in quarters in zip-lock freezer bags so that we only defrost as much as we need at any one time.*

**\*\*\*\*\***

# COUNTRY STYLE VANILLA ICE CREAM

**4 eggs**
**2 ½ cups sugar**
**4 cups whipping cream**

**2 tbsp. vanilla**
**¼ tsp. salt**
**5 cups milk (approx.)**

Beat eggs until foamy in large mixing bowl. Gradually add sugar and beat until thickened. Add cream, vanilla and salt and mix thoroughly until sugar dissolves and all ingredients are incorporated. Pour into ice cream maker. Add milk to fill line. Freeze as directed. Makes about 4 qts.

*We make so much of this ice cream recipe that we cannot afford the time or the trouble of a hand-cranking machine with a pretty wooden tub. We leave that to the purist and buy one of the inexpensive (about $20) electric ice cream makers that are so plentiful on the market. At the rate we make ice cream, one of these machines lasts about two years. Let's see. I've been married to Paul about twenty six or so years. That means that we have gone through about ...*

*This is a great recipe for ice cream and we usually stick to making vanilla, but changes can be made for other flavors by adding fresh fruit as it is made. Do not sweeten the fruit. The natural sweetness of the added fruit is enhanced by the ice cream and vice versa.*

\*\*\*\*\*

## WHIPPED CREAM TOPPING

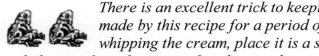

**2 cups whipping cream**
**3 tbsp. sugar**

Place cream in a deep-sided bowl and begin whipping with an electric beater on low speed. Add sugar slowly as the cream begins to obtain some volume. Whip until thick and sugar is incorporated into mix.

*Serve with any and everything. Many of the recipes in this section use whipping cream to add to their presentation as well as give a delightful boost to their flavor. To suit your needs and taste, adjust the amount of cream used as well as the sugar.*

*There is an excellent trick to keeping the whipped cream made by this recipe for a period of up to a week: After whipping the cream, place it is a strainer over a bowl and place in the refrigerator for about an hour or more. The liquids remaining in the cream will drain and become separated from the cream.*

*Doing it this way helps maintain the cream in a whipped state for from several days to a week (if it lasts that long at your house. Paul is constantly making inroads into any we have in the refrigerator). Place the cream in a tightly sealed container and refrigerate. This will help the cream retain its full flavor and whipped state.*

*****

## STELLA'S LEMON ICE

2 tsp. lemon rind
2 cups sugar
4 cups water

¼ tsp. salt
3/4 cup lemon juice (fresh squeezed)

Grate lemons onto sugar. Add water and salt. Heat slowly until sugar dissolves. Bring to a boil and boil for five minutes. Cover without stirring to avoid crystallization. Chill and then add lemon juice. Churn or still freeze.

 *This is an extremely refreshing light desert to have during the summer. It is an excellent replacement for ice cream (which, to be honest, can be a little heavy in hot weather).*

 *An alternative to the lemon flavoring, is freshly squeezed grapefruit juice. Try it. We like both.*

 *Small dabs of defrosted frozen fruits such as raspberries can be put on top the ices for added zest. Use only small amounts so as not to detract from the ices original flavor. Paul likes to add just a splash (no more or the ices will melt) of Grand Marnier.*

  *An excellent way that the lemon ice can add panache to a several course dinner with special guests, is to serve a slight amount (perhaps two large tablespoons) of the ice in a sherry glass between courses. Surprisingly, this will "cleanse the palate," i.e. separate the flavors between the disparate tastes of the two courses.*

\*\*\*\*\*

# CHEESECAKE

### Crust:

1 ½ cups graham cracker crumbs
4 tbsps. ground almonds, pecans or walnuts

2 tbsps. sugar
½ cup melted butter

### Filling:

1 ½ lb. soft cream cheese
1 cup sugar
1 tsps. vanilla

3 tsps. lemon juice
1 tsp. lemon zest
4 eggs

### Topping:

1 pt. cold sour cream
½ cup sugar

½ tsp. vanilla
Cinnamon

Combine crust ingredients and press into 9" spring form pan. Bake at 350 degrees for 10 minutes.

Beat cheese in large bowl until creamy. Gradually add sugar, vanilla, lemon juice and zest. Add eggs one at a time and beat on medium speed until fluffy.

Pour into pan and bake in 350 degree oven for 35 minutes. Turn off heat and let cool in oven for 30 minutes with the oven door open.

Combine sour cream, sugar and vanilla and whip for 10 minutes until foamy. Spoon on cake and bake in 250 degree oven for 10 minutes. Sprinkle with cinnamon and cool.

Chill for at least two hours before serving.

 *Leave the topping off and this cake freezes beautifully. Remember to let it thaw slowly in the refrigerator before serving. Once it is defrosted, add topping.*

**\*\*\*\*\***

## *FROZEN PEACH (OR ANY FRUIT) DESSERT*

**2 cups frozen, sugared peaches    1 tbsp. sugar**
**½ cup fresh whipping cream**

Partially defrost peaches and pour whipping cream over them.
Remember to only partially defrost fruit. Sprinkle with sugar and serve.

 *This sounds like a relatively simple dessert and it is. The beauty of it is its simplicity. It is easy to make and the results are great! The cream adheres to the partially frozen peaches and freezes ever so slightly so that the combination tastes just like fresh peach ice cream.*

*For special occasions, add a tbsp. of peach brandy to each serving to give it a little more zest. As with seemingly every other desert with fruit and cream, Paul likes to add Grand Marnier.*

 *Paul likes Mississippi peaches this way and I sort of agree with him. However, you can use this process with other fruits and berries. Apricots, nectarines, strawberries, blueberries, blackberries, and raspberries work equally as well.*

*I like to take advantage of the Hancock County Farmers' Market or the U-Pick fields in our area to get my fresh peaches or, for that matter, any of the fruits and berries when they come into season. This way you are sure they have ripened just before being picked.*

*I then freeze them with some sugar and add a little lemon juice (½ tsp.) and place them in serving size freezer bags and use them all year long. These make nice, quick desserts for those of us who are always in a rush to prepare a quick meal.*

\*\*\*\*\*

## CHOCOLATE MOUSSE

| | |
|---|---|
| 8 oz. sweet or semi-sweet chocolate | 3 egg white |
| ¼ cup dark, strong coffee | ¼ cup finely ground sugar |
| 3 oz. softened unsalted butter | Whipped cream |
| 3 egg yolks | Fresh or frozen raspberries |
| 1 cup heavy cream | |

Melt chocolate with coffee in the microwave very slowly so as not to scorch. Remove from microwave and stir until smooth. Beat the butter into the chocolate and add the egg yolks one by one and mix thoroughly. Let the chocolate mixture cool.

Beat the heavy cream until thick. Beat egg whites and add the sugar in a sprinkling fashion until the whites form stiff peaks. Fold the chocolate, whipped cream and the egg whites together gently. Turn the mouse into a serving bowl or individual serving dishes.

Chill several hours. Serves 6 to 8.

 *This is a truly elegant and tasty dessert. Excellent for company or just for yourself. It makes you and your company feel very special.*

  *We like to garnish each serving with a dollop of whipped cream and fresh or frozen raspberries. For some reason, raspberries are always an excellent accompaniment to chocolate. This is somewhat strange, because the strong flavor of raspberries tends to overpower most other flavors and, therefore despite being delicious, must be used very sparingly.*

*Strawberries are also a good garnish. We prefer to use fresh strawberries.*

\*\*\*\*\*

## MAYONNAISE ICE CREAM

**8 oz. heavy whipping cream**     **2 tbsp. mayonnaise**
**3 tbsp. sugar**                      **1 tbsp. whipping cream**
**1 28 oz. can fruit cocktail**       **1 tsp. sugar**

Whip the cream, incorporating the sugar, until stiff peaks form in the cream. Place fruit cocktail (do not drain) in a large bowl and fold in the whipped cream and mayonnaise until uniformly blended. Place mixture in a shallow pan and freeze.

Serve with a small amount of cream drizzled over the ice cream along with a sprinkle of sugar. Serves 6 to 8.

*****

## PAUL'S TURNOVERS

**1 double recipe of your favorite pie dough**
**Various jams, jellies or preserves**

Roll out pie dough and cut into circle. Drop a teaspoon or so of jam on dough on each circle. Moisten outside of circle with water, fold in half and seal around the edges using the tines of a fork. Pierce the dough with a fork to allow steam to come out and bake at 375 degrees until dough browns.

Remove from oven and cool.

 *Paul's mother made these for him when he was small. She would make them with scraps from a pie dough when she and Paul's older sister were cooking in the kitchen on a Saturday. Eating them brings back a lot of his chidhood memories. I have to watch him, he often eats the turnovers before they have properly cooled and he gets his tongue burned by the hot jam!*

*****

## PIZZELLES

1 doz. eggs
2 cups sugar
1 ¾ cups Crisco oil
1 ½ tsp. vanilla

4 oz. anise oil
4 tbsp. anise seeds
½ cup anise liquor
5 cups flour

Beat eggs. Add sugar and beat again. Add oil, vanilla, anise oil and seeds, liquor and beat until smooth. Gradually add flour until the mixture once again becomes smooth. If batter thickens, thin with liquor.

Follow baking instructions that came with your Pizzelle iron.

*These are Christmas treats. We make them weeks in advance of holidays and weddings and store them in large empty coffee cans. It is part of my heritage and is an important part of the occasions overall ambience. They are a staple we bring out when we have people stopping by during the holidays and serve them with coffee, tea or ice cream.*

*What is surprisingly nice is that their flavor gets better with age and also that they seem to keep forever.*

**\*\*\*\*\***

## PINEAPPLE WALNUT CAKE

### Cake

| | |
|---|---|
| 2 cups cake flour | 1 tsp. vanilla |
| 1 ¾ cups sugar | 2 eggs |
| 2 tsps. baking soda | 20 oz. can crushed pineapple |
| 1 cup chopped walnuts | with juice |

Mix above ingredients and pour into an ungreased 9" x 13" pan. Bake at 350 degrees for 45 minutes.

### Walnut Icing

| | |
|---|---|
| 1 soft stick butter | 1 tsp. vanilla |
| 8 oz. soft cream cheese | ½ cup finely chopped walnuts |
| 1 ½ cups powered sugar | (optional) |

Mix above ingredients until smooth and ice the cake while it is still warm. Refrigerate cake after icing. Serve when completely cooled.

*****

## PINEAPPLE CREAM PIE

| | |
|---|---|
| 1 cup sugar | 6 tbsps. cornstarch |
| 2 ½ cups boiling water | 4 egg yolks |
| 1 can crushed pineapple | ½ cup butter |

Bring above ingredients to a boil over medium heat until thickened. Remove from heat and chill before pouring into a prepared piecrust. Beat eggs white for a meringue topping. Brown topping slightly in hot oven.

*****

## CARMEL FLAN

| | |
|---|---|
| **1 cup sugar** | **4 egg yolks** |
| **2 cups milk** | **½ tsp. vanilla extract** |
| **1/8 tsp. salt** | **Nutmeg, fresh** |

Caramelize ½ cup sugar and divide among four individual custard dishes.  Combine milk, sugar and salt.  Add egg yolks and beat well.  Add vanilla and beat again.  Pour mixture into custard dishes and sprinkle with fresh nutmeg.  Set custard dishes in pan of hot water and place in oven and bake at 300 degree for 20 to 30 minutes.

Chill and serve.  Serves four.

*Do not overcook flan.  A fast test is to insert a butter knife in the flan and, if it comes out clean, flan is done.*

\*\*\*\*\*

## KRUSCIKI

| | |
|---|---|
| **6 egg yolks** | **3 cups flour** |
| **3 tbsp. grated orange rind** | **1 cup powdered sugar** |
| **½ tsp. salt** | **Vegetable oil for frying** |
| **½ pt. sour cream** | |

Beat egg yolk and add orange, salt, cream, 2½ cups flour and sugar and mix well. Add remaining flour and work by hand to form a soft dough. On a floured surface, roll a quarter of the dough at a time to about 1/8" thickness. Cut dough in 3" long rectangles and cut a slit in center of each. Pull ends though each center and make bows. Fry in oil at 375 degrees until lightly browned (30 to 40 seconds). Drain on paper towels. Cool and sprinkle with powdered sugar.

*This last recipe is for my Polish Grandmother. She made these wonderful delicate cookies whenever we expected company. I loved these cookies and still do. They are excellent to serve with coffee or tea or just as a quick snack. Be careful, they are best made on days with low humidity as they absorb moisture easily.*

*Stella and Paul La Violette*

*If you liked this book,*
*why not order more copies for your dearest friends*

| ORDER FORM | BLUEBERRY PEACHES, RED ROBIN PIE |
|---|---|

MAIL ORDERS TO:  Annabelle Publishing
Post Office Box 87
Waveland, MS  39576

Blueberry Peaches, Red Robin Pie @ $18.95 x _____ copies  =  _____

Shipping and handling @ $5.50 per copy  =  _____

TOTAL  =  _____

Please make check or money order payable to: Annabelle Publishing

NAME _____

ADDRESS _____

CITY_____ STATE _____ ZIP_____

| ORDER FORM | BLUEBERRY PEACHES, RED ROBIN PIE |
|---|---|

MAIL ORDERS TO:  Annabelle Publishing
Post Office Box 87
Waveland, MS  39576

Blueberry Peaches, Red Robin Pie @ $18.95 x _____ copies  =  _____

Shipping and handling @ $5.50 per copy  =  _____

TOTAL  =  _____

Please make check or money order payable to: Annabelle Publishing

NAME _____

ADDRESS _____

CITY_____ STATE _____ ZIP_____